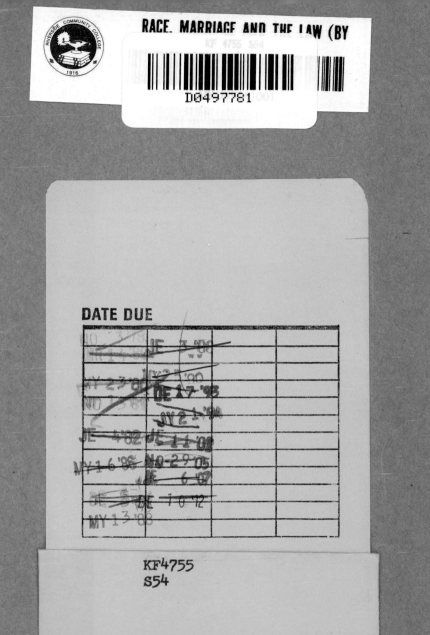

DATE DUE

NO 3 '78	JE 3 '00		
MR 14	MY 28 '00		
MY 23 '80	DE 17 '98		
NO 13 '81	MY 21 '94		
JE 4 '82	JE 11 '00		
MY 16 '86	NO 29 '05		
	JE 6 '07		
JE 5	DE 10 '12		
MY 13 '00			

Race, Marriage, and the Law

RACE
MARRIAGE
and the
LAW

Robert J. Sickels

University of New Mexico Press
Albuquerque

©The University of New Mexico Press, 1972.
Manufactured in the United States of America.
Library of Congress Catalog Card Number 72-86815.
International Standard Book Number 0-8263-0256-4.

For Alice and Dorothy

Contents

1

Court and Taboo

Loving v. Virginia

A simple announcement by Chief Justice Warren, "Judgment reversed," signaled the end of the crime of racial intermarriage in the United States and the end of harassment, wearisome litigation, and banishment for Richard and Mildred Loving. On June 12, 1967, in the appeal of *Loving v. Virginia*,[1] the United States Supreme Court unanimously held Virginia's antimiscegenation[2] law void under the clauses of the Fourteenth Amendment of the Constitution which provide that "No State shall . . . deprive any person of life, liberty, or property, without due process of law; nor deny to any person within its jurisdiction the equal protection of the laws," putting the Lovings and interracial couples generally on an equal footing with others in all sixteen states where antimiscegenation laws were in force.

"I feel free now," said Mildred Loving when she learned of the decision. "It was a great burden." The twenty-seven-year-old Negro woman, at a press conference called by her American Civil Liberties Union attorneys in Alexandria, across the Potomac River from Washington, said she never doubted that the Supreme Court would decide in favor of her marriage to Richard Loving. "It feels so great," said he, a white construction worker six years her senior. "But it's hard to believe. I still don't believe it. . . . For the first time

I can put my arm around her and publicly call her my
wife." ³ After nine years and ten days of fugitive marriage,
the Lovings had won a new status, the freedom to live and
travel together without the threat of imprisonment. Their
three children, six to eight years old, were never told very
much about their parents' legal difficulties, and now, as they
approached the age at which children learn of adult matters
despite parental precautions, they would be spared a discov-
ery that their father and mother were criminals in their native state and they, the children, bastards by law. When a
newspaper reporter asked Richard Loving what advice he
would give his children later on about marriage, he replied,
"I think I'd leave it up to them. . . . Let them decide for
themselves." As for himself, "If I'd lost this time, I was coming right back and try five years later." ⁴

Following five years of exile in the District of Columbia,
where no law forbade interracial marriage or cohabitation,
the Lovings had returned in 1963 to their farm and relatives
in Virginia hill country in Caroline County, between Fred-
ericksburg and Richmond, and worked from then on with
the American Civil Liberties Union to win a reversal of
their conviction. They remained there by informal agreement with their local prosecuting attorney, at peace with
their neighbors of both races while their case was argued
before various courts of appeals. But the hazards of their situation were never far from consciousness: in neighboring
Essex County, where one of the Loving children attended
school, the prosecutor threatened the parents with arrest
and trial if he caught them in his bailiwick.⁵ From 1963 to
1967 their personal struggle was a test case used by organized minorities and sympathetic liberals to challenge a
legal principle that seemed to mock the national ideals of
liberty and equality. Personally, the Lovings' story is one of
frustration and perseverance from court to court. For the
larger group—those who were hurt or might have been hurt

by antimiscegenation laws, or those such as the staff of the American Civil Liberties Union who gave legal assistance— it is an interesting tale of justice delayed.

1954–1967: "One bombshell at a time is enough"

In *Loving* v. *Virginia* the Supreme Court took a step that would have been thought bold ten or fifteen years before. It brought down the antimiscegenation laws of Virginia and fifteen other states in an uncompromising, unanimous decision. When it came at last in 1967, the decision was honored by egalitarians as the close of explicit racial discrimination in American statutory law, but for those who had followed the progress of the miscegenation issue in the courts it also marked the end of years of abortive litigation. On three occasions, all after 1954, in the years following *Brown* v. *Board of Education*,[6] when it was most receptive to complaints of unequal treatment under law, the Supreme Court either rejected miscegenation cases outright or accepted a case for review and disposed of it on sufficiently narrow grounds to avoid the hard question of the constitutionality of a ban on interracial marriage.

Only a few months after *Brown*, the Court refused without dissent to review a conviction of miscegenation in Alabama. *Jackson* v. *Alabama* was an ideal test case for the opponents of antimiscegenation legislation because the question of constitutionality had been squarely presented in appeals within the state and rejected by the judges of Alabama. Perhaps this was a reason why the United States Supreme Court chose not to take the case: to decide it on grounds more modest than those later employed in *Loving* v. *Virginia* would have been difficult.[7] A year later the Court, again without dissent, turned aside the case of *Naim*

v. *Naim,* in which the question of constitutionality was not
set out distinctly. After sending it back for clarification of
the record, the Court ruled in March, 1956, that the case
lacked a properly presented federal question.[8] "One
bombshell at a time is enough," one member of the Court is
reported to have said, with *Brown* v. *Board of Education* in
mind.[9] In 1964 the Court decided the interracial cohabitation case of *McLaughlin* v. *Florida* without ruling on the
constitutionality of the state's law against mixed marriage.[10]
In each case the Supreme Court could have found the laws
in conflict with the demands of the Fourteenth Amendment,
but invoked its lawful power, instead, to choose its own bat-
tleground.

When the ruling finally came in *Loving* v. *Virginia,* the
legality of antimiscegenation laws was not a live issue any
more. The force of twelve years of decisions on other aspects of racial equality and the precedent of *McLaughlin* on
the adjacent issue of interracial cohabitation left little doubt
that the Court would decide solidly against antimiscegenation laws when it elected to confront them. The Court had
prudently delayed decision until the legality (although not
the desirability) of interracial marriage was no longer controversial. The course of its rulings on mixed marriage
closely paralleled its school prayer decisions: first the Court
turned away an appeal on procedural grounds, much later it
accepted a case which allowed a narrow decision accompanied by some broad hints about the treatment the larger
claim might receive when presented directly, and not long
afterwards the culminating case was decided almost anticli-
mactically.[11]

Newspapers reported the *Loving* decision routinely, with
a minimum of editorial commentary. In Congress, where a
number of outspoken critics of the Court are always to be
found, and particularly in the Senate, where the nomination
of Thurgood Marshall as the first black member of the Su-

preme Court was debated in the weeks following *Loving*, there was almost no mention of the miscegenation issue. In the lengthy nomination hearings in the Judiciary Committee from July 13 to July 24, 1967, which are by tradition an invitation to air grievances about recent Court decisions, only this brief exchange touched upon miscegenation:

> SENATOR THURMOND: Do you know of any specific evidence relating to antimiscegenation laws that was presented to the Supreme Court in *Loving* v. *Virginia* which contradicted the historical evidence of the Commonwealth of Virginia that the 14th Amendment was not intended to affect antimiscegenation laws, and if you don't know of such evidence, how do you justify the Court saying that the historical evidence was not conclusive?
>
> JUDGE MARSHALL: I am not familiar with the case. I am only familiar with the opinion. I did not read the record in that case.[12]

That the decision was directed against offending states rather than another branch of the national government and that it was not expected to have much effect on intermarriage in the South, where strong racial folkways are a deterrent in the absence of legal prohibitions, are two additional reasons for the restrained reaction in Washington. In these respects too the school prayer litigation runs parallel: it was state action the Court interdicted, and its rulings were freely ignored in some parts of the country.

The strain of conservatism in the Court which decided *Loving* v. *Virginia* can be observed in another civil rights decision handed down the same day. In *Walker* v. *Birmingham* a divided Supreme Court allowed the jailing of Martin Luther King on a contempt charge under a patently unconstitutional state injunction.[13] The facts were simple. A group of black civil rights advocates applied for a parade permit for a peaceful street demonstration in Birmingham from Public Safety Commissioner Eugene "Bull" Connor. His reply was, "No, you will not get a permit in Birmingham, Alabama, to picket. I will picket you over to the City Jail." Commissioner Connor's refusal was reinforced by a county court injunction forbidding the group to participate in street parades without a permit. Rather than fight these rulings through the local courts, King and his followers went ahead with their march and were arrested. A bare majority of the Supreme Court held that the group should have challenged the injunction in the Alabama courts. Chief Justice Warren and Associate Justices Brennan, Douglas, and Fortas held in dissent that the underlying ordinance and the injunction were unconstitutional on their face, that King and his colleagues had properly tested them by holding their demonstration and remaining in Birmingham to submit to the courts, and that the majority was "elevating a state rule of judicial administration above the right of free expression guaranteed in the Constitution."

While the majority showed concern for procedural regularity over questions of individual rights in *Walker* v. *Birmingham,* more fundamentally they seemed anxious to dampen the enthusiasm of civil rights activists in the interests of domestic tranquillity. In 1967 the members of the Court, like a good many private citizens, were perceptibly more conservative on race issues than in previous years. By decision day on June 12, the long summer of racial violence was well under way. On controversial questions such as the lawfulness of demonstrations the Court was circumspect and divided. But on the *Loving* issue it could afford a symbolic nine-to-nothing gift to the black community with little risk of white outrage. In timing its consideration of the problem and then, in 1967, in disposing of it the Court remained undivided, from first to last. Polls showed, and perhaps the Court sensed, that by now few whites still believed that blacks really cared to intermarry.

The Court's conservative strategy

The measured approach of the Supreme Court to sensitive issues conserves its powers for work it can do effectively and prevents a waste of good will in premature consideration of questions which will be manageable a decade or two later. When it is first posed, a problem such as the legality of miscegenation raises dreadful fears in many people that a change in legal tradition will spark a revolution in social behavior. After a time, when the inevitability of a change in the law has been intimated by an increasing tempo of litigation in the lower courts and a stepwise advance to the central issue by the Supreme Court, the objecting public, perhaps reflecting on the history of school desegregation or prohibition, becomes more confident of the impotence of legal pressures alone in a hostile environment and less concerned about new rules of law.

We can predict a pattern of behavior with respect to such issues: a broad new rule is demanded; the courts act cautiously for fear of provoking an ugly public response; in the debate between reformers and conservatives that ensues, an increasingly realistic assessment of the limited role of law emerges and reduces the interest of all parties in the outcome of the legal struggle; meanwhile considerations of legal and moral consistency make a decision unavoidable in the long run; when it comes, the decision is neither feared nor carried out at the levels originally anticipated.

On less volatile issues the Supreme Court enjoys more freedom of action because the only people who are seriously interested in the outcome are those materially affected. Where the structure of interests is pluralistic, the Court can dispense its punishments and rewards with no real concern about the anger of citizens and the retributions of Congress. But there are some issues, of which miscegenation is one,

capable of raising anxieties among a mass of spectators.
Lunch-counter integration in the South was another: the response of the Supreme Court was avoidance of all crucial
questions in case after case, until it was rescued by state
and federal legislation that removed the need for a direct
constitutional decision. Whether to allow American citizens
to travel to Communist countries is another, and the Court's
response has been a deliberate and parsimonious series of
decisions elaborating the rights of travelers without deciding any broad constitutional points. Lunch-counter integration, travel to forbidden lands, and miscegenation all involve strong taboos. The average man with no urge to eat at
a lunch counter, to go to Cuba, or to marry into another
race may yet feel threatened very personally by this liberty
in others, as we shall note in the next chapter. Other people's unrestrained behavior jeopardizes his identity and
self-control. Popular concern about student morals is very
much of this nature. Therefore one can expect the Court to
act conservatively in cases involving student rights.

An illustration from another area of the law may serve to
clarify the strategy of the Court in handling delicate public
issues. There is some pressure now on all levels of government in the United States to grant rights to homosexuals
equal to those of heterosexuals, including the removal of
laws punishing homosexual relations between consenting
adults. At the moment there is a wealth of legal precedent
on equal rights, mainly concerning blacks, that could be put
to this purpose by the courts. The taboo against homosexuality, which is a reflection of the anxiety of the average man
about his own sexual identity, is as strong as any in the culture and stronger even than the fear of miscegenation. For
the Supreme Court to implant a homosexual bill of rights in
the Fourteenth Amendment, though a logical extension of
honored principles, is unlikely today. It is low on legal
priority lists, to say the least. But perhaps in 1975 and again

in 1980 the Court will turn aside cases raising the issues, decide a secondary issue in 1985, and then, when the legal aspects of homosexuality are no longer controversial—let us say in 1990—it will hand down a ruling for homosexuals as comprehensive, and as quietly received, as *Loving*.

In the story of miscegenation and the law the Supreme Court's limited role has been to keep debate alive and to intervene at the right time with a benediction for a consensus already taking hold in the legal community. *Loving* v. *Virginia* was offered as an admonition to the larger, more prejudiced community, a gentle reminder of the distance between social reality and moral ideal.

This politic behavior of the Supreme Court does not please standpatters or the activists who would have the justices shed their dark robes for burnished armor and their guerrilla maneuvers for dragon-slaying outright. But, conceiving themselves as political realists, the justices have employed delay and controlled response as their "third alternative to martyrdom or to knuckling under." [14] In the case of miscegenation, the Court understood it must contend with an unsympathetic public and expect an unpleasant reaction to any precipitate ruling it might make in favor of racial mixing.

As the next two chapters indicate, popular feeling against miscegenation runs deep. As depicted below the surface by psychologists and psychiatrists, prejudice about racial mixing has the profundity of a genuine taboo. Expressed in opinion polls and public utterances, it is pervasive and sharp. *Loving*, it is clear, was decided for racial and intellectual minorities.

2

The Miscegenation Taboo

The rewards of a caste system

In the United States the taboo against racial intermarriage lends support to a caste system of superior and inferior social and economic roles for whites and blacks, who characteristically take their places in this system as nameless members of skin-color groups in which they are fixed for life. Members of the white group, and often the members of the black group too, reinforce one another's caste beliefs by deed and by word, setting out a pattern of roles rewarding enough to be assured by social sanction in the face of egalitarian norms and firm enough to be learned generation after generation intact.

Caste attitudes are so deeply held, within the privileged group, so widely shared, and so useful socially and psychologically that the abrupt removal of legal barriers to interracial marriage is generally considered likely to bring about no greater change in marital patterns than might occur if the states did away with their rules against marriages between first cousins or uncles and nieces. The Supreme Court could approach the Lovings' case with the knowledge that a liberal decision would provoke the approval of members of the more educated public, the broad disapproval of the public at large, and—by 1967—intense reactions in very few people in either stratum.

There are rewards of caste more obvious than the psychic, but not more potent. The economic, for example: a pool of labor stands ready to perform unattractive tasks—such as domestic labor, garbage collection, sweeping, dishwashing, stoop labor, and odd jobs—at low wages and often without effective minimum wage protection; and whites inherit the better jobs with a reduced risk of competition. A dramatic clue to the impact of caste on the job market is the fact that the median income of black high school graduates is below that of whites with only eight years of school, and the income of black college graduates is less than that of white high school graduates.[1]

Caste also benefits the white male with a wider choice of sex partners than it allows black males. The white man may undertake marriage with whites and sexual relations with both whites and blacks without much awkwardness, but ordinarily black males are confined to marriage and sexual relations within their race. It might be noted that the advantage of the white male may be more theoretical than real if his ability to enjoy his larger selection of partners is inhibited by inner conflicts about sex, particularly with white women.

Frequently for the white male, and perhaps increasingly for the black, sexual relations with a woman of another race are regarded as a challenge, a test of manhood imposed by social pressure as much as an act of personal choice. But this sexual advantage will diminish if white women become more permissive toward white males, or for that matter toward males of both races.

The psychological rewards of caste are more subtle. Racial prejudice in general and miscegenation beliefs in particular are sturdy mental braces for the white person who has a normal or an abnormal complement of needs, doubts, and anxieties. His prejudice is a cheap, effective short-run tonic for many frustrations, the functional equivalent of gin or marijuana and equally resistant to eradication by preaching. With a strong dose of prejudice, a member of the dominant caste can give order and meaning to much of the world around him, construct a more pleasing image of himself, and slough off uncomfortable thoughts onto members of the lower caste, all without guilt or morning-after maladies.

Generalizing is a way to give meaning to the confusion of the environment. Without generalization, when each observation is unique, there is chaos; with it—at best the inclusive formulas of a Newton or an Einstein—the world makes sense. A perfectly rational man would hope not to overgeneralize and shut out new information, but the average man willingly trades some rationality for some peace of mind. He may indulge in primitive overgeneralization (perhaps from a small sample, perhaps from none at all) about the bestial urges of blacks in the ghetto in order to come to grips with the morning's news about urban unrest. As a child he probably gained some power of explanation by jumping to animistic conclusions about the self-direction and life of his rubber ball or the moon in the sky. If primitive thinking as an adult has the added function of justifying his morally questionable behavior ("my treatment of Negroes is quite generous, considering their deficiencies"), it is most likely to thrive and to lead to rigid stereotyping.

A firm and pleasing self-image, too, can be derived from racial prejudice as a part of the process of marking off groups with which to identify and not to indentify: the other side of taking pride in one's associations and at the same time in oneself, is feeling that groups for which one does not have a sense of belonging are alien, undesirable, and in the limiting case of caste, wholly inferior in worth and status. Miscegenation puts the white man's identity in jeopardy because the threat to the integrity of his race is a threat to his own psychic survival. (In some cases the taboo may have the related function of covering fears about the racial purity of one's own family tree.)

To the white man whose personality is largely defined by caste, the question "Would you want your daughter to marry one?" is real. His dread of racial contamination is as powerful and personal as the fear of homosexuality is for some others: in each case the fears define and sustain the man. If he imagines that desegregation of schools and public accommodations will lead to miscegenation, the white with caste beliefs will dread civil rights in general. Myrdal contends that rhetoric about the dangers of miscegenation is a rationalization for the maintenance of social and economic discrimination against Negroes. But the loathing of racial mixture is not to be dismissed as a pretext for the continuation of segregation. When whites suffer status anxieties, the pain is eased perceptibly by an assertion of superiority over blacks in ways that range from discriminatory epithets to mayhem and assassination, all to clarify the boundaries of the group and the self. Attitude tests confirm that status consciousness and racial prejudice go together, and suggest that the antimiscegenationist has much at stake in his protestations.

Still another benefit derived from a racial taboo is the displacement of menacing emotions upon the lower caste. Racial prejudice generally is a subconscious projection, upon a safe and convenient target group, of wishes and fears too powerful for the ordinary member of the dominant caste to handle literally. It is mental theater, more pleasing than one's real self and real world. Certainly the miscegenation taboo cannot be explained as "human nature," because specific taboos against intermarriage are not universal, but the mechanism of projection seems to be present in some form in the behavior of every human being, and its appearance as the miscegenation taboo depends only on predisposing factors.

The black person is an inkblot test for the prejudiced white, a relationship that comforts whites, informs psychologists, and torments blacks. Projections have strikingly similar features in color-caste societies around the world: dark-skinned males are believed to be unusually violent and virile and thus likely rapists, and black women are considered alluring and promiscuous. In South Africa, the sex life of Negroes is a matter of fascination and concern to the white population. It is the black people who are assumed to be the rapists and the miscegenationists, although in reality it is the whites who cross color lines for sexual relations in nearly every instance there and in the United States, and it is overwhelmingly the whites who are aggressive and exploitative in sexual and other human relations in both countries. In such places, violence and sexual urges in whites are projected upon the blacks as a release from a burden of socially unacceptable impulses.

Projection frequently appears in the form of scapegoating. Target groups vary but the behavior is uniform: an outgroup is used for the displacement of aggressive or guilt-laden impulses. It is a mistake to oversimplify the miscegenation taboo as the deliberate perversity of committed racists. Since it is not under his full conscious control, the taboo can be neither adopted nor abandoned by the white person at will; it cannot be explored by psychologists except by slowly stripping away layers of protective rationalization in therapy or by tests which keep the purpose of the questions from the subject and elicit unguarded responses; and its dynamics are unlikely even to seem plausible to members of the general public who harbor the taboo and are accordingly disposed to fend off thoughts which threaten to expose the strong emotions involved.

The prejudiced man's image of the scapegoat is not always one of inferiority and degradation. Traditional German caste attitudes, for example, have ranged from fear and suspicion of the demonic qualities of Jews to feelings of intellectual and moral superiority toward Slavic peoples.[2] In America the Negro takes on deficiencies and excesses simultaneously: he is a Slav, in a manner of speaking, but sexually demonic. The prejudiced white person knows that not every —or not any—black of his acquaintance is dull, ugly, dirty, and diseased, but assumes these to be essential racial characteristics that will pass to the young, including the offspring of a miscegenous union. In the mind of the white, a member of the pariah group cannot shed the stereotype even if his attainments and behavior are the very opposite of the despised model. Similarly the stereotype can adhere to a light-skinned person who is black by legal definition because of a black grandparent.

Of all the attributes of an inferior group, the most feared is its power to pollute. A prejudiced white person may shrink from the contamination of a black handshake— although the touch of a black servant is benign. Eating, perhaps because of the symbolism of breaking bread with equals and its association with the intimacy of the home and family, is a ritual open to contamination of this kind, which explains some of the emotion in whites' resistance to the desegregation of lunch counters and restaurants in the South, although here again the black servant or cook is not considered a contaminator. But the ultimate pollution and ultimate challenge to the dominance of the superior racial caste is intermarriage. All of the psychic force mobilized to avoid contact with dirt and excreta is available for the maintenance of barriers against racial contamination in a caste society.

In a place like the United States where there is a good deal of sexual inhibition, the outgroup which assumes the unwanted impulses of the dominant group becomes sexually exciting. Where sex is repressed and at the same time promoted with mystery and enchantment, it should be no surprise that the shadowy Negro is a carrier of projected sexual lust.[3] Negroes have a role similar to that of witches in Navajo culture who draw the blame for others' personal failures, or to the biblical goat that takes the sins of the people on its head and suffers banishment into the wilderness. In England, where Pakistanis strongly oppose intermarriage with whites, Pakistani newspapers contain articles and letters asserting that white women do not make good wives because they are slovenly, domineering, and, as one can tell from their low necklines and brief skirts, likely to be unfaithful.[4]

The miscegenation taboo is destined to lose some of its power if sex taboos in general lose theirs, since the projection of sexual lust onto others bestows rewards only if the impulses feel wicked in the first place. If sexuality is more easily accepted, intermarriage will increase. But illicit miscegenation will decline because it is supported by racism and segregation: social distance between castes fosters projection and scapegoating, and feeds the white man's fantasy of the oversexed outgroup. Sex lines are crossed more, illicitly, where caste lines are most rigid, where whites have made blacks sexually attractive by displacing highly charged impulses upon them.

"The attraction is a condensation of many pregenital and genital feelings of the individual," writes a psychoanalyst.

> In calling a Negro a child of nature, simple, lovable, without ambition, a person who gives way to his every impulse, white men have made a symbol which gives a secret gratification to those who are inhibited or crippled in their instinctual satisfactions. . . .[5]

And it is not simply the attraction of white men to black women: there is evidence from psychoanalysis and from more commonplace sources that white women find black men unusually attractive. Sometimes this impulse takes the projected form of masochistic fantasies of rape: the inner temptation becomes an external threat.[6]

In the white man's mind, particularly in the South, the danger of rape is accompanied by an idealization of white women. Raised amidst exaggerated respect and adoration of white womanhood, the white male may experience some difficulty enjoying a loving, satisfying sexual relationship with a white woman of his social rank or one higher, his wife not excepted. His frustrations are camouflaged under homage to the ideals of white womanhood, a sort of protesting too much that is common in everyday life, as in the surface hypermasculinity of a man who has deep doubts about his manhood, or the strict pacifism of an essentially aggressive, hostile person. The white man's urges may be satisfied, however, in relations with a "bad" or "inferior" person. Raising his wife on a pedestal and slipping out the back door for covert sexual relations with a black woman are psychologically consistent, mutually reinforcing actions, however differently they may strike the moralist. The white woman is an inadequate sexual partner because she is rhapsodized and rhapsodized because she is an inadequate sexual partner. For her part, the white woman may entertain rape fantasies because she too is sexually deprived. Her own protestations of purity may mask an attraction to blacks, whose mythic prowess has been celebrated by whites, and her fears of black sexual aggression may help to hide a history of white sexual aggression against blacks, as active toward black men as it is toward black women. The same phenomenon of closely guarded high-caste women and sexually exploited low-caste women has been found in India.[7]

W. J. Cash describes the idealization of Southern women:

> Merely to mention her was to send strong men into tears—or shouts. There was hardly a sermon that did not end with tributes in her honor, hardly a brave speech that did not open and close with a clashing of shields and flourishing of swords for her glory.[8]

Compare this college fraternity toast of a generation ago, from Alabama:

> To woman, lovely woman of the Southland, as pure and as chaste as this sparkling water, as cold as this gleaming ice, we lift this cup, and we pledge our hearts and our lives to the protection of her virtue and chastity.[9]

The white woman is "cold" and untouchable. Sexual thoughts about her are inappropriate unless veiled as a flourishing of swords, sexual acts exact a toll of guilt, and the myth protects the white man from his own habits and attitudes without requiring him to put sexual matters entirely out of mind. He can defend white womanhood from the threat of black sexuality and, more to the point, from his own sexual drive too. The display of admiration and protectiveness for white women is in fact a barrier raised by whites against themselves, though ostensibly against Negroes. It is a way of thinking shared strongly by white women, who are in general more prejudiced than men against Negroes.[10]

Although the taboo against intermarriage applies to white males and black females as well as to black males and white females, the corollary prohibition of sexual activity is limited to black males and white females in the minds of most whites. The accident of becoming the parent of a dark child outside of marriage is a more obvious embarrassment to a white woman than to a white man. Since parentage can be disavowed by a white father, if he is cognizant of it, he in no way jeopardizes the purity and status of his caste.

The misperceptions and hostility underlying racial prejudice are widespread enough not to be endangered by the test of reality. Prejudice is socially convenient, comforting, and readily taught to children. Once the caste and taboo are in place and social distance is attained, the perpetuation of a system of prejudices is relatively simple. For some people with personality problems, maintenance of the caste system is vital.

Forms of prejudice

It is useful to distinguish between two forms of prejudice against Negroes: in one case a family, a social class, or a community instructs a white child in the lessons of black inferiority and the child becomes a prejudiced adult with respect to Negroes but not necessarily in other respects; in the second case a family and perhaps a class or other group treats a child in such a way that he develops a generalized prejudice that applies incidentally to Negroes. Not infrequently, the two forms are compounded in one person.

The separability of specific and general forms of racial prejudice was demonstrated some years ago in an analysis of the attitudes of white West Virginia miners. Some of the men were consistently prejudiced, some were consistently unprejudiced, and most were inconsistently willing to work side by side with Negroes below ground but unwilling to mix on the surface. The conclusion of the study, which is not beyond criticism, is that the three-fifths with inconsistent views were behaving in ways specifically determined by community norms, while those with consistently prejudicial views are best understood in psychological terms, as having prejudiced personalities.[11] Had they been tested, the former might have scored normally on ethnocentrism and authoritarianism scales, or normally for people of the miners' social class, and the latter might have scored high.

Many people who are prejudiced against Negroes are prejudiced against other racial and ethnic minorities and also have attitudes such as rigidity, conventionality, punitiveness, and deference to superiors that are associated with authoritarianism. But tests so far suggest that southern whites are not more authoritarian than nonsoutherners. The

greater incidence of racial prejudice in the South depends
on specific socialization in black-white caste attitudes.
Southerners tend to display feelings on zoning and miscegenation, for example, that vary sharply according to
whether Negroes are involved or some other racial or ethnic
group.[12] General prejudice is not regional, however: people
with severe internal conflicts susceptible of projection on
the environment in the form of racial prejudice are as common in the northern regions of the United States as in the
southern.[13] (Still it is curious that on the Gallup Poll "worry
indexes" compiled in 1966, a greater proportion of southerners than others admit to being "very worried" about each
issue mentioned: Vietnam, prices, strikes and labor problems, economic depression, world war, and "racial problems." [14] Perhaps more testing is in order.)

What appears as a lonely, disquieting, deviant projective
mechanism in one community may in other circumstances
be a shared belief that comfortably binds the members of
the dominant caste.[15] An ethnocentric or authoritarian person will exploit a milieu of racial prejudice, and a person
predisposed to tolerance will tend to soften the standards of
the prejudiced community.

The distinction between forms of prejudice is in no sense
final. Early students of the authoritarian personality emphasized its deviant character. Lately there has been some good
research on lower-class authoritarianism, and some of the
intolerance and lack of perspective of the authoritarian have
been traced to social phenomena such as the limited experiences and education of members of that class.[16]

The authoritarian personality

In any community, some children will be raised in a way
that is likely to give them lasting disabilities, ready to sur-

face as generalized prejudice. One family environment in particular has a fairly predictable outcome in prejudice: the authoritarian, inegalitarian home in which the father rules rigidly and harshly, the mother is moralistic, submissive, and self-sacrificing, and the child learns quiet obedience under threats of parental displeasure and punishment. Parental affection is given out sparingly as a reward for the renunciation of instinctual pleasures.[17] In a home of this kind it is difficult for a child to have secrets from his parents and to develop a mind and conscience of his own or even to express wishes and fears. Because his impulses are curbed by his parents, the child is likely to project them onto others. If they are not permitted to appear directly, his urges surface indirectly in fantasy.

The more coercive his home, the greater the disparity between the child as he presents himself to others and the child as creator of fantasy. To all appearances he is a faithful and willing disciple of his parents' obtrusive morality. Underneath, however, instead of love for his parents and identification with them, there brews a pervasive animosity.[18]

A part of the fantasy world of the child of authoritarian parents concerns the image of his parents themselves. A natural hostility toward unpleasant parents may be too much for the child to accept, in which event he will cover it over with a heavy icing of love and respect. The same is likely to be true of sexual feelings toward his parents, which the anti-sexual moralism of the home drives deep underground. Raised in this setting, a boy is inclined to express his anger toward his father in obedience, affection, and a life of rugged masculinity, and his thwarted affection and resulting hostility for his mother in terms of asexual respect and admiration. After a while all of the real angers and desires show up in the form of fantasies directed at safe targets such as depressed minorities. If resentment toward his father is

prohibited, the white authoritarian can release it upon Negroes. If sexuality toward his mother and other revered
women is prohibited, he can discover pure sexuality in Negroes. Rigidly self-controlled, he develops a lifetime habit of
discharging his impulses evasively rather than in direct hu-
mane activities.

The two sides of the world of fantasy—unusually warm,
accepting attitudes toward parents and raw impulses projected onto others—help to explain the easy oversimplified
loyalty to one's own family, community, or race and the
disdain for outsiders in this kind of child and in the adult he
becomes. He depicts those around him grossly and unreal-
istically in ways that bring relief from unwanted impulses.
He is intolerant of ambiguity and prefers stereotyping to accuracy of description, which might challenge his make-be-
lieve world. It has been found that if a pollster approaches
him, he is quite unlikely to offer a "don't know" response.

Yet this kind of person is always insecure in his membership in the privileged caste and must expend a good deal of
energy demonstrating his acceptability. The values that
matter are not safely internalized in the form of a conscience, but remain outside in parents and parentlike authority figures, so that the most commonly accepted authorities, the purveyors of fixed conventional morality, attract
the allegiance of this person, who never enjoyed the luxury
of identifying with his parents and winning his autonomy
and who therefore never quite matured. Males of this sort
tend to work at suppressing all traits of femininity, females all
traits of masculinity, in a wearing lifelong struggle to conform to the polarities limned by their parents.

A code of moral conduct supplied by authority figures in
the privileged caste, preferably by strong dominant men,
can be all the more respected when the rumblings of one's
own immoral impulses are sensed. And self-assurance is in-
tensified by a conviction that an identifiable group such as

Negroes embodies all the violations of the code. This prejudiced soul has an either-or outlook: he does not like fence-
sitters. The chauvinist's "America—love it or leave it" slogan
reflects his own feeling that all members of the in-group
must accept the code and assimilate totally or be cast out.
His stereotyping of Negroes as animal-like, instinctual, and
unrestrained and of whites as respectable and good shows
the same mechanism at work. If his authority figures permit
discrimination and aggression against blacks, he leaps to the
attack.

The miscegenation taboo is a part of this pattern. The boy
who has been held in check by a stern father and deprived
of freedom to develop his own masculinity, who is inhibited
by the antisexual morality and exaggerated respect for
womanhood of his authoritarian home, displays a tenderness
toward his mother and "respectable" white women in general that conflicts with his anger and his desire for sexual expression. He may always find it difficult to have both sexual
and tender, loving impulses toward the same woman. In a
roundabout way, his thwarted urges in childhood and adult-
hood lead to total acceptance of prevailing stereotypes of
asexual whites and hypersexual blacks. In accepting the taboo
and teaching black men to avoid white women, the white
man tells himself not to harbor a lust for good white women
and, *au fond,* for his good mother. It is no wonder that
"motherfucker" is America's most potent projective maledic-
tion.

The entire pattern of prejudice and taboo in the authoritarian person may in general terms be understood as a response to anxiety. One's own faults are seen in others,
whether they exist there or not. Negroes are accused of feeling superior, for example—a wonderfully unrealistic projection in most instances. Because they have less effective ways
of overcoming frustration than others have, broadly prejudiced people anger quickly and childishly, and displace

their anger instead of dealing straightforwardly with the source of their frustration.[19] The authoritarian is also likely to have an unusually strong interest in sexual matters, transmuted into punitive attitudes toward the supposed transgressions of others, and he has unrelieved concern about ethnic and racial pollution.

Altogether, the social, cultural, and psychological supports of racial prejudice and the miscegenation taboo are real enough to promise much continuing public opposition to intermarriage. There are impulses in the dominant caste which are all too readily displaced on blacks. In Europe it has been the Jews, notably, who have drawn society's surplus emotions and have been regarded as filthy and lecherous in the bargain. Everywhere people can be found for whom ethnic and racial prejudice is a way of life, who are chauvinistic, denigrating lower peoples around the world, and typically religious in the narrow sense of *dis*believing the creeds of others. Nowhere are the combined passions against outsiders and in support of insiders better summed up than in a passage from the famous 1948 "vigorous belief in the principles of white supremacy" speech of G. Harrold Carswell, unsuccessful Nixon nominee for the United States Supreme Court, linking patriotism, racism, and sexuality in unwittingly rich imagery:

> . . . by the eternal stars in the folds of Old Glory, we shall not ever sit idly by while the sneaking efforts of the Communist snake slithers its way into the vitals of our nation. Our answer to them is and will always be, "Keep your hands out of the American Eagle's nest." [20]

Prejudice, in short, is a powerful generalized component of the personality of many people as well as a specific pattern of behavior learned in the community.

Black attitudes toward miscegenation

Blacks' attitudes toward interracial marriage, as spectators and participants, differ only in degree from those of whites. Psychological studies confirm the findings of public opinion polls that there is a deep strain of opposition to miscegenation among Negroes. But it must be noted that some accounts of *the* view of Negroes have exaggerated the consensus. A frequently quoted volume entitled *A Negro's Faith in America*, for example, has helped calm the fears of whites and lent support to the thesis of Myrdal and others that blacks have more important social goals than miscegenation. In it Spencer Logan writes, "One barrier to a closer drawing together of the white and the Negro races in America has been the misconception on the part of many whites that the Negro desires amalgamation." He adds, "Speaking as a Negro, I know that most Negroes do not desire sexual relationships with white women." [21] But a very different view is expressed by black sociologist Calvin Hernton in his book *Sex and Racism in America*. Hernton argues that whites fear and blacks desire racial mixing with equal vigor. He finds an obsessive sexual attraction of black youths to white girls, and contends that black men attempt sexual relations with white women by force or persuasion notwithstanding the occasional threat of death and mutilation, just as some white men, at far less risk, rape or seduce black women. A good share of the racial violence in the country, Hernton says, consists of sexual atrocities directed at black men and women by whites who will not permit miscegenation without a mortal struggle, except as the exploitation of blacks.

If there is indeed any significant attraction of black males to white females, it might well be exacerbated by the representations of white feminine glamour in the products of

Hollywood and Madison Avenue. Real white girls may be
remote, but pictures are inescapable on television, book
jackets, and packages in the store, and in movies, maga-
zines, and newspapers. The high pressure look-but-don't-
touch sexuality of adult white society is certain to have an
impact on blacks—one evidence of which in the past has
been the market for skin bleach and hair straighteners in
the ghetto. But Negroes are no more likely to be fully aware
of their own feelings about miscegenation than whites. The
defensive and projective patterns found in people generally,
and in high degree in authoritarians, discourage self-knowl-
edge. Negroes on the whole seem to have personalities more
authoritarian than whites, even when education, occupa-
tion, and other variables of status are held constant. In fact,
a test of black college students revealed higher levels of authoritarianism among the female freshmen, on the average,
than among the highly authoritarian inmates of San Quen-
tin Prison.[22] It might be expected that Negroes would develop qualities such as conventionality, respect for tough-
ness, and the submissiveness and aggressiveness that go
together in the authoritarian personality. The surprise is
that the adversities of black life in the North and South do
not produce even more insecurity, anxiety, and attendant
pathological responses.

A good number of Negroes do accept the common white
assessment of their race as a pariah group, and accept also
the traditional view of their native Africa as a dark continent in need of civilizing from afar. This acceptance is an
effective support of the caste system by a people bereft of
tradition and identity. Some Negroes play the role they are
handed—inferiority, supersexuality, and so forth—and feed
white prejudice in the process. This role playing is more
than prudent dissimulation. Blacks who have been taught
shame for their color and their culture, and have obtained
some small solace by imitating whites, may choose to value

white middle-class aspirations over identification with their brethren. It is only lately that black pride and a reassessment of the heritage of the mother continent have taken hold in a substantial cross section of the black community. Its advocates in the past, including W. E. B. DuBois and Marcus Garvey, were heard by a minority. Today blacks have an option of picking an identity other than that cast upon them by whites.

A forced role of sexual athlete, with inhibitions on its exercise ranging from miscegenation taboos to the psychic castration of welfare dependency, unemployment, and underemployment, gives black men less animal pleasure than whites sometimes presume. The confusion and self-contempt that ensues is measured by the high suicide rates of young urban black men, by their homosexuality—preferably with white partners—and by the turning of aggressions outward in homicide.[23] It also takes the form of revenge against whites through an acting out of the myth. Taking up with a white woman can prove a splendid way of lashing back at an inegalitarian society. It is the opposite of Uncle Tom's role, in a sense, yet it is a way of life dictated by white stereotypes, because the rebel is a mimic too.

Perhaps Myrdal's is the most balanced assessment after all, for the mass of Negroes: "No educated or intelligent Negro could ever agree that, because of his race, it should not be possible for him to marry as he pleases. He is against that. I don't think, however, that—as a practical thing—intermarriage is much on his mind. It is more on the white man's mind than the Negro's." [24]

Partners in interracial marriage

Breaking the miscegenation taboo by marrying a person of another race takes a special mental makeup for blacks

and for whites. It may be that the pattern resembles that
discovered by J. D. Barber among state legislators: instead
of a normal distribution of psychological strengths and
weaknesses, he found the legislators abnormally strong-
minded or abnormally weak. The former labored deliber-
ately and effectively toward goals they had chosen; the
latter frequently sought in legislative membership the
self-esteem they lacked in private life.[25] In the case of miscegenous marriage, some seem to have the advantage of autonomy and strong will, others seem to engage in miscegenation precisely because they have disabilities such as those
of the prejudiced authoritarian. Some marry because they
are able to rise above the taboo, others because of the taboo.
One or both marriage partners may seek revenge, the immature white by dealing a blow to parents whose approval or
disapproval continues to guide and circumscribe his life, the
black partner by getting back at white racism with the
greatest taunt of all. The two use each other in a way that
makes a lasting marriage improbable.

Even if contracted for more propitious reasons, an interracial marriage in this age and place has the power to bring
out neurotic tendencies in the partners. The evidence of
psychiatrists favors this conclusion, although it should be
kept in mind that they treat troubled people and therefore
are unlikely to take account of the healthy in their generali-
zations. Black psychiatrist Thomas Brayboy in particular
has been cited for his belief that miscegenous marriages
constitute an invitation to act out character deficiencies.
They have little room for affection. They involve deep-
rooted mental illness. As an illustration, he describes the
case of the left-wing white woman who married a black na-
tionalist, breaching both racial and ideological lines and
pooling her aggressions and vengefulness with his in a marriage without love or understanding. Her father and her
husband, each in his way, were both intense racists.[26] In

general, stressful and disorganized family life has been found to be associated with a higher-than-average frequency of marriage outside one's nationality or race.

It is ironic that a neurotic should be identified by his deviation from a norm such as racial purity, which is kept alive by immature and elaborately defensive attitudes, but as long as racism is a societal norm many miscegenationists will be moved by neurotic drives. If and when the norm changes, healthy interracial marriages built on love and respect may predominate.

One study of interracial marriages in the District of Columbia, with a more representative sample than the psychiatrists', indicates that many miscegenationists are "emancipated persons" who by acculturation and personal contact have shed the prejudices and other qualities which inhibit interracial marriage and are good prospects for long and happy matrimony. They rank low on scales of promiscuity, demoralization, and rebelliousness.[27] Others have come to the same conclusion, having found relatively large numbers of strong-willed, independent-minded intellectuals, bohemians, and religious and political radicals among the racially intermarried.[28]

The obvious problems of living out an interracial marriage are enough to tax sturdy people. Gross discrimination, from insults to violence, is less common than it was a few years ago, but nearly all interracial couples report that it is hard to endure the inescapable staring of the hostile and the merely curious. The families of the spouses are not likely to be much more supportive than the general public: the white partner's family typically refuses to meet the black partner, simply because of race, and the black partner's family may or may not do the same, depending more on the individual in question than the color of his skin. The Negro community as a whole tends to condemn interracial marriage, but to accept some of the white partners. White spouses are reported

passing as black in order to fit more easily into black society. Of course some interracial spouses were isolated from
their families before marriage and married in secret. Their
continued estrangement may be a boon to everyone.

Roger and Berta M——, who helped overthrow Mississippi's durable mixed-marriage law in 1970, enjoyed the support of his parents, but hers were strongly opposed to marriage to a white. Since the wedding, the pair have had to
bear the curiosity of neighbors, newsmen, shoppers, and
others, but the families are reconciled.[29]

Children of racially mixed marriages have special problems of identity. In this country they are considered Negroes, but with fewer credentials than others for full membership in the black community. Whether the interracial
couples have fewer children, and whether if so it is due to
concern for the children, concern for themselves, or simply
the higher median age of such spouses, is not known. The
sparse evidence is contradictory. If the facts were known,
child production might be a good test of marital adjustment
and the psychological soundness of miscegenous marriage in
the world today.

One suspects that a good many contemporary interracial
marriages have been undertaken by prejudiced people who
accept the racial myths whole: the Negro may feel that a
white partner is a good catch, and the white may retreat to
the supposed black beast because he is unable to enjoy sexual contact with "respectable" whites. One psychiatrist,
Charles Smith, shares this suspicion, but with a note of opti-
mism. He has found that a large share of the misfortune in
interracial marriage comes from the white's stereotyped attitudes about blacks, and that with a stint of therapeutic de-
mythicizing the white spouse's insight and the quality of the
marriage can both be improved.[30]

What interracial couples share with the entire community

is a serious interest in the issue of miscegenation and in the public policy which inhibits or allows it. It is an issue that touches raw nerves.

Therefore, attacking the legal supports of the antimiscegenation taboo was a venture the Supreme Court could contemplate only with some misgivings. Yet the force of popular opposition to racial mixing was itself the best assurance that little of the psychic energy invested in this prejudice would be displaced upon the Court. By 1967 the public, and presumably the Court, knew that no radical alteration in the incidence of interracial marriage was in the offing, decision or not. The Court, with some impunity at last, could satisfy the egalitarian demands of those who spoke for the conscience of the community.

3

The Climate of Opinion

If raw public sentiment were all the Supreme Court weighed in predicting the popularity of an impending decision, to strike down state antimiscegenation laws might have seemed an unqualified mistake. But in the politics of judicial review, the rule of one man, one vote does not hold, because some opinions matter more than others. Mass attitudes were against the Lovings' claim, clearly; but among the educated minority, including the members of the Court, a measure of tolerance prevailed. In fact several publics with different opinions confronted the Court, among them the general adult population, bearing its heavy load of racial prejudice; judges who had ruled and written on miscegenation over the years, willingly upholding race laws in every case but one; scientists who had debated questions of racial equality and racial mixing; churchmen and other liberal leaders of opinion; and the members of the Court themselves, who were accountable to their own consciences.

The feelings of the general public are reflected in opinion polls, speeches, and popular writings—even in the words of such venerable authorities as former President Harry Truman, who once told a reporter who asked if he thought racial intermarriage would ever be popular,

> I hope not. I don't believe in it. What's that word about ten feet long? Miscegenation?
> Would you want your daughter to marry a Negro? [1]

And Lincoln:

> Judge Douglas is especially horrified at the thought
> of mixing the blood of the white and black races.
> Agreed for once—a thousand times agreed. . . .[2]

> I do not understand that because I do not want a
> negro woman for a slave I must necessarily want her
> for a wife. My understanding is that I can just let her
> alone. . . . I have never had the least apprehension
> that I or my friends would marry negroes if there was
> no law to keep them from it, but as Judge Douglas and
> his friends seem to be in great apprehension that they
> might, if there was no law to keep them from it, I give
> him the most solemn pledge that I will to the very last
> stand by the law of this state, which forbids the marry-
> ing of white people with negroes.[3]

And a Shakespearean villain:

> Even now, now, very now, an old black ram
> Is tupping your white ewe. . . .
> Zounds,   sir,   . . .   you'll   have   your   daughter
> covered   with   a   Barbary   horse,   you'll   have
> your   nephews   neigh   to   you,   you'll   have   coursers
> for cousins, and jennets for germans.[4]

But for the most part, public apologists for the taboo have
been simple southern white supremacists. Moderates who
share the taboo, and many liberals who do not, have preferred to keep their silence on a subject of such delicacy. In
the press it has been discussed very little. The Motion Picture Production Code, Hollywood's self-censorship system,
forbade the theme of miscegenation entirely until 1965.[5]

White supremacist rhetoric

The dominant theme in southern antimiscegenation rhetoric has been that social contact between the races—in public schools, for instance—leads to the twin evils of sexual relations and mixed offspring: miscegenation and "mongrelization." In the past there was a tendency to make the point with unashamed malice. Today antimiscegenationists are often more genteel, pledging good faith and charity before sounding the alarm for racial separation. A sampling of the old declamations and some of the new will illustrate the tragicomic flavor.

In the wake of the Civil War, the Knights of the White Camellia labored to maintain the *status quo ante bellum,* aided by stringent laws on the order of Mississippi's, which provided life imprisonment for miscegenationists. Candidates for membership in the Knights of the White Camellia were required to answer such questions as:

> Do you belong to the white race?
> Did you ever marry any woman who did not, or does not, belong to the white race?
> Do you promise never to marry any woman but one who belongs to the white race?
> Do you believe in the superiority of your race?
> Are you willing to take an oath forever to cherish these grand principles, and to unite yourself with others who, like you, believing in their truth, have firmly bound themselves to stand by and defend them against all?

Recruits who responded favorably to the questions were read a charge urging racial purity:

. . . Our main and fundamental object if the MAIN-
TENANCE OF THE SUPREMACY OF THE WHITE
RACE in this Republic.

. . . . If we were to admit persons of African race on
the same level with ourselves, a state of personal relations would follow which would unavoidably lead to
political equality. . . . The man who is good enough to
be our familiar companion is good enough also to participate in our political government. . . .

There is another reason, Brothers, for which we condemn this social equality. Its toleration would soon be
a fruitful source of intermarriage between individuals
of the two races; and the result of this *miscegenation*
would be gradual amalgamation and the production of
a degenerate and bastard offspring, which would soon
populate these states with a degraded and ignoble population, incapable of moral and intellectual development and unfitted to support a great and powerful
country. We must maintain the purity of white blood,
if we would preserve for it that natural superiority
with which God had ennobled it.[6]

In an uninhibited essay published in Texas at the turn of
the century, one W. C. Brann wrote that Negroes should be
presented the alternative of emigration or annihilation.

We have tried the restraining influence of religion
and the elevating forces of education upon the negro
without avail. We have employed moral suasion and
legal penalties; have incarcerated the offenders for life
at hard labor, and hanged them by the neck in accordance with statutory law. We have hunted the black
rape-fiend to death with hounds, bored him with buck-
shot; fricasseed him over slow fires and flayed him
alive; but the despoilment of white women by these
brutal imps of darkness and the devil is still of daily

occurrence. The baleful shadow of the black man hangs over every Southern home like the sword of Damocles, like the blight of death—an avatar of infamy, a decree of damnation. . . .

Drive out the "nigger"—young and old, male and female—or drive him into the earth! It may be urged that the "good negro" would suffer with the bad. It is impossible to distinguish the one from the other until it is too late. It were better that a thousand "good negroes"—if so many there be—should suffer death or banishment than that one good white woman should be debauched.[7]

In 1947 Senator Theodore Bilbo of Mississippi, a modern Brann, concluded his book, *Take Your Choice,* with this call to action:

We are today standing at the crossroads, and there are but two roads ahead. Separation leads to the preservation of both the white and Negro races, to a future which belongs to God. Mongrelization leads to the destruction of our Nation itself.

Take your choice—separation or mongrelization. The America of tomorrow—white or mongrel? Let us pray that Almighty God will guide our feet upon a road to a white America which will continue to lead the world in civilization and culture.[8]

The Senator's solution was embodied in a bill "for the voluntary resettlement of American Negroes in their fatherland, West Africa," first introduced in the United States Senate in April 1939, providing for the purchase of up to four hundred thousand acres near Liberia and an American military government to supervise resettlement, the construction of roads and towns, and the administration of grants-in-aid to the settlers, and then withdrawal in favor of a civil terri-

torial regime. Brann and Bilbo were equally certain that
blacks and whites would mix destructively if blacks were
not removed from the land.

Even now some old-fashioned crudity of expression occurs in publications of the Ku Klux Klan, as compiled by the
House Un-American Activities Committee in 1966 and 1967:
number seventeen among "Fifty Reasons Why You Should
Be a Member of the Original Ku Klux Klan" is "Because it is
opposed to intermarriages between niggers and White
people." [9] In the constitution and laws of the KKK there appears an invitation ". . . to share with us the glory of per-
forming the sacred duty of protecting womanhood; to maintain forever the God-given supremacy of the White race; to
commemorate the holy and chivalric achievements of our
fathers"; and so forth. [10] From the White Knights of the Ku
Klux Klan of Mississippi comes this newsletter (with names
deleted by the committee):

> Questions all White Citizens of Lauderdale County
> and the City of Meridian should ask your neigh-
> bors. . . .
> 10. Who is the white nigger lady who is dating a nig-
> ger sailor. She works at °°°.
> 11. Who is the white waitress at °°° who can't keep
> her hands off the white nigger boy who works in the
> °°°.
> 12. Who is the white lady and her daughter who oper-
> ate a °°° on °°° who is so fond of the nigger in the
> kitchen. [11]

Similarly, Atlanta Klansman and lawyer J. B. Stoner won
national attention with his address in St. Augustine for the
National States Rights Party in 1965, which culminated in a
blunt lesson in zoology and economics:

> The nigger is not a human being. He is somewhere
> between the white man and the ape. We don't believe

in tolerance. We don't believe in getting along with
our enemy, and the nigger is our enemy. Every time a
nigger gets a job, that's just one more job that you
can't have.

You notice the niggers are singing, "I love everybody." They sure do love everybody, and especially
our white women. What the nigger really wants is our
white women.[12]

A motif of this tradition is the imminent peril of miscegenation if people are left to themselves. One frightened white
described a 1965 civil rights march on Montgomery, Alabama, as a mélange of "sexual maniacs, dope addicts, mentally deranged communists, and a few well meaning brain-
washed people with no understanding of human decency."[13]
Many pages of the *Congressional Record* have been filled
with stories of the sexual implications of civil rights, high-
lighted by tales of prostitutes demonstrating in nuns' habits.
But note the new tone of gentility and the abstention from
flagrant racism, accomplished in part by the use of Communists as secondary scapegoats to draw censure away from the
primary scapegoats, the blacks. "There were four distinct
and usually identifiable groups intermingled and partici-
pating in a common effort but each for its own motives,"
said an Alabama Congressman:

One group was the Alabama Negro who participated
to help secure rights and privileges which he felt had
been withdrawn from him illegally. And there are
many instances where this has been so—especially historically. This is not universally so in Alabama,
however—only in isolated areas and none of these
areas recently.

A second group are the do-gooders—those from outside our State who have no personal interest or involvement but who, out of compassion for those whom

they are convinced need help and, although misin-
formed and misguided as to both the full facts and how
those whom they seek to help can best be helped,
come and participate in the marches, demonstrations,
and even serious civil disturbances. This group, for the
most part are serious, sincere, educated people such as
the clergy, nuns, teachers, and other professional people. While their purpose may be noble, to a large extent they defeat their own aims because they worsen
the condition they seek to improve. . . .

These two groups, however, make up only a small
part of the total effort. Both of these groups are in fact
being victimized and used as unknowing tools of the
other two groups involved. . . .

The third group, also a tool being used by the fourth
group, are human flotsam: adventurers, beatnicks,
prostitutes, and similar rabble. . . . The fact is that
they are recruited to be full-time demonstrators. They
are promised $10 per day, free room and board and all
of the sex they want from opposite members of either
race. Free love among this group is not only condoned;
it is encouraged. It is a fact and their way of life. Only
by the ultimate sex act with one of another color can
they demonstrate they have no prejudice.

. . . Drunkenness and sex orgies were the order of
the day in Selma, on the road to Montgomery, and in
Montgomery. There were many—not just a few—
instances of sexual intercourse in public between
Negro and white. . . .

Who . . . is the one or group that puts these groups
together—that gives it cohesiveness, strength, money,
and direction? Who or what can weld this diverse
group together into a formidable force that can—and
has—overcome? The answer is this: the Communist
Party. . . .

Mr. Speaker, I implore this body to cast aside all
prejudice by color—pro or con. Forget race and look at
all the facts objectively. Recently the American public
has been made colorblind to the point that black
makes red white. America must substitute reason and
fact for emotion. We must wake up before it is too late.
It may be too late now.[14]

Gruesome affidavits sworn by citizens and police of Alabama and spread in the *Record* alleged such sights as
drunken priests, girls with no underpants, fondling in
churches, sexual relations in the streets, and white girls and
black men holding hands, not to mention one crowning spec-
tacle of mass interracial urination at the command of a black
leader.[15]

Some modern defenses of racial purity make their point
without evoking the specters of rape, orgy, and subversion.
An essay by Herbert Ravenal Sass in the *Atlantic Monthly*,
"Mixed Schools and Mixed Blood," illustrates a gentler
style. Sass too is convinced that social mixing leads to miscegenation. He appeals to Yankee conscience not to impose a
second Reconstruction upon the South, confident that
northern ardor for integration will be dampened by an understanding of its consequences. The mere fact that he
writes for the *Atlantic Monthly* suggests that Sass is aiming
as much for the mind as for the heart and groin.

For the democratic public school is the most critical
of those areas of activity where the South must and
will at all costs maintain separation of the races. The
South must do this because, although it is a nearly universal instinct, race preference is not active in the very
young. Race preference (which the propagandists mis-
call race prejudice or hate) is one of those instincts
which develop gradually as the mind develops and
which, if taken in hand early enough, can be prevented
from developing at all.[16]

Race shapes culture, Sass argues: in most endeavors pure-blooded nations have surpassed the nations of mixed blood. The United States, Canada, Argentina, and Uruguay alone among the nations of the Western Hemisphere have maintained a high degree of racial purity and a high level of civilization, he contends. Discrimination? Of course. A nation achieves greatness by discriminating. It should protect its gains by continuing its racial distinctions.

> Many well-meaning persons have suddenly discovered that the tenets of the Christian religion and the professions of our democratic faith compel us to accept the risks of this hybridization. No one who will face up to the biological facts and really think the problem through can believe any such thing or see the partial suicide of the white race in America (and of the Negro race also) as anything other than a crime against both religion and civilization.

Sass takes pains to assure his readers that the Negroes of the South are well cared for by the whites. Many southern customs bearing on race relations which outsiders regard as harsh and cruel he considers no more than defenses thrown up against the abolitionists who wish to alter a benign system and Africanize the region.

The South has "separated" blacks, but it has not "segregated" them like reservation Indians:

> The South has not done that to the Negro. On the contrary, it has shared its countryside and its cities with him in amity and understanding, not perfect by any means, and careful of established folk custom, but far exceeding in human friendliness anything of the kind found in the north.

Arguments of this nature strike many northern whites and Negroes in any part of the country as exercises in duplicity, even satiric humor. To many white southerners, Sass's remarks have the ring of plain truth.

It is well to note that the intensity of the opposition of
some whites to miscegenation is demonstrated in deed as
well as word. The taboo is reaffirmed from time to time in
the reports of lynching in the South and violence against interracial couples in northern suburban communities.[17]

Public opinion polls

The rhetoric reported here does not itself prove anything
about American public opinion on racial purity. Together
with opinion polls demonstrating that a large though diminishing majority of the people in the country oppose miscegenation, however, this sample proves to be a fair representation of popular prejudices. The KKK gives expression to
feelings harbored by masses of white people in America.

A Gallup Poll in late 1968 revealed that 72 percent of
American adults disapproved of marriage between whites
and nonwhites, 20 percent approved, and 8 percent had no
opinion.[18] If some of those interviewed gave a proper answer instead of a sincere one, even the response of 20 percent approval is inflated. The same poll showed men to be
somewhat more tolerant than women of mixed marriage.[19]
Two years before, a Harris Poll indicated that 88 percent of
adult whites would object to dating by their teenage child
and a Negro, and 79 percent would be upset by the marriage of a close friend or relative and a Negro.[20] And the
year before that, in 1965, the Gallup Poll reported that 48
percent of the adults in the nation approved of *criminal* antimiscegenation laws, 46 percent disapproved, and 6 percent
had no opinion.[21] In general, then, around the time of the
Loving decision, a strong majority opposed miscegenation
and about one-half felt the threat of imprisonment appropri-

ate in support of the taboo. The liberal views expressed by the lawyers for the Lovings before the Supreme Court clearly went against public opinion.

Judicial opinion

Another source of views for the Court to consider in 1967 was case law. But cases, like popular opinion, offered no comfort to anyone contemplating the destruction of antimiscegenation laws. Weightier in authority for legalists and more accessible than the views of mass man, many of these arguments were reiterated in the briefs for Virginia and for the Lovings in 1967. Over the years, the great majority of judges who have written about miscegenation have opposed it, vehemently.

Judges of state and federal courts, in the course of deciding causes involving miscegenation and other racial matters, have written essays on the meaning of race that rank among the most poetic in the literature. On great moral issues, a judge in the common-law tradition turns teacher, historian, philosopher, and minister of the gospel to bring the full burden of civilization to bear on the dispute at hand. The result is obiter dictum: a lecture that goes beyond the needs of the case in order to shed as much light as possible upon it.

In law, there is a timeless quality in the rhetoric of racial separation. Consider this passage from a conservative federal court reviewing plans for school desegregation. Certain details aside, it could be 1860 rather than 1960:

> What has integration itself accomplished in the lands where it has existed for centuries?
> In the colonial period France had two promising colonies in America: Quebec on the frozen icebound shores of the St. Lawrence and Haiti, Guadalupe et al.

in the West Indies. In Quebec there was no integration. The 4,000,000 French Canadians are a religious, orderly people. In Haiti the integration had been but shortly allowed when one race destroyed the other. In Puerto Rico, integration and amalgamation early became the order. In the Southern States the white and the former slave each retained his racial integrity. Is the Puerto Rican any better advanced than the Southern Negro? No Southern Negro has ever shot up the halls of Congress, killed the President's guard and sought his life. One was integrated and the other was not.

Cuba was integrated at an early period. Costa Rica has no racial amalgamation or integration. All is peace, progress and beauty in Costa Rica, while blood and discord flow in Cuba.

Integration has not helped either race. It has retarded the development of every land where it has occurred.

Why rush it here? [22]

The judge's opinion goes on with an imaginative tale of a benevolent slave culture in the United States and the conversion of blacks to Christianity, which induced good behavior under threat of damnation.

When the fratricidal strife was on between the states, when brother sought the blood of brother and eleven states walked out of the Union, every man available went into the army. There was nobody left to run the plantations but the slaves and the mistress of the great house. She took these slaves and they ran the plantation. She knew how to do it. They also had a Negro foreman who also knew how to do it and the South carried on. Production kept up. They had plenty on which to live. Sherman's army found an abundance

as he marched through Georgia. Four years the blood-
letting went on. More than two million black men run-
ning the plantations under the direction of their mistress never once took her life or molested her person.
Such a story of loyalty's devotion was never before told
nor since witnessed. They wouldn't molest that mistress.[23]

Emancipation and Reconstruction disrupted the peace and
racial harmony of the South, in the court's view of history.
Blacks were taught by scalawags and carpetbaggers to turn
on their benefactors, and in parts of the South there were
fears of racial war.[24]

Today, in the judge's opinion, the danger is that people
will be persuaded by their experiences as children in integrated schools to risk amalgamation, which he considers a
disaster wherever it has occurred.

> The white Southerner is proud of the fact that he
> has many Negro citizens among his neighbors who also
> have racial pride and do not look forward with any
> special desire to amalgamation of the two races. But an
> integration in the schoolroom taking the small child in
> grade 1 on up until he finishes high school places the
> current side by side in a closer channel than it has
> heretofore been. . . .
> Take Southern Europe and Northern Europe. In
> Northern Europe the different tribes and nationalities
> have married and inbred into their own tribes and
> kindred tribes—what the cattleman would call line
> breeding which makes purity of race. In breeding a
> cow by line breeding and care you produce a valuable
> animal, sometimes worth thousands of dollars. . . . In
> Southern Europe instead of line breeding there has
> been cross breeding. . . .
> Those who favor racial integrity do not look with

favor upon the result. We do not say that the people of
Sicily and the fringes of the Mediterranean are not
equal to the people of the northern belt of the continent, but we do say that they are not superior.[25]

This uncompromising point of view is exceptional in the
writings of the modern federal judiciary, but a century or
even a third of a century ago it was a commonplace, as a review of case law demonstrates. A good starting place is an
1857 decision, *Dred Scott* v. *Sandford,* in which the Supreme Court of the United States went well beyond the demands of the controversy before it to declare Negroes incapable of holding citizenship in the United States and to find
an Act of Congress, the Missouri Compromise of 1820, unconstitutional for its supposed encroachment upon the property rights of slaveholders over their slaves. In his opinion,
Chief Justice Taney cited antimiscegenation statutes in effect at the time of ratification of the Constitution as evidence of the "perpetual and impassable barrier . . . erected
between the white race and the one which they had reduced to slavery. . . ."[26]

From the same period comes this reminder that racial
prejudice has a long history above the Mason-Dixon line as
well as below it. This is an opinion of the Supreme Court of
Pennsylvania in a case concerning segregated railway cars
and a number of other things:

> The right to separate being clear in proper cases,
> and it being the subject of sound regulation, the ques-
> tion remaining to be considered is, whether there is
> such a difference between the white and black races
> within this State, resulting from nature, law and cus-
> tom, as makes it a reasonable ground of separation.
> The question is one of difference, not of superiority or
> inferiority. Why the Creator made one black and the
> other white we do not know, but the fact is apparent

and the races are distinct, each producing its own kind
and following the peculiar law of its constitution. Con-
ceding equality, with natures as perfect and rights as
sacred, yet God has made them dissimilar, with those
natural instincts and feelings which He always imparts
to His creatures when He intends that they shall not
overstep the natural boundaries He has assigned to
them. The natural law which forbids their intermarriage and that social amalgamation which leads to a
corruption of races is as clearly divine as that which
imparted to them different natures. The tendency of
intimate social intermixture is to amalgamation, contrary to the law of races. The separation of white and
black races upon the surface of the globe is a fact
equally apparent. Why this is so it is not necessary to
speculate; but the fact of a distribution of men by race
and color is as visible in the providential arrangement
of the earth as that of heat and cold. The natural separation of the races is, therefore, an undeniable fact, and
all social organizations which lead to their amalgamation are repugnant to the law of nature. From social
amalgamation it is but a step to illicit intercourse, and
but another to intermarriage. But to assert separateness is not to declare inferiority in either; it is not to
declare one a slave and the other a freeman; that
would be to draw the illogical sequence of inferiority
from difference only. It is simply to say that, following
the order of Divine Providence, human authority
ought not to compel these widely separate races to intermix. The right of such to be free from social contact
is as clear as to be free from intermarriage. The former
may be less repulsive as a condition, but no less entitled to protection as a right. When, therefore, we declare a right to maintain separate relations as far as
reasonably practicable, but in a spirit of kindness and

charity, and with due regard to equality of rights, it is
not prejudice, nor caste, nor injustice of any kind, but
simply to suffer men to follow the law of races established by the Creator himself, and not to compel them
to intermix contrary to their instincts.[27]

In 1869, a year after the adoption of the Fourteenth
Amendment, a Georgia judge forbade the marriage of a
Frenchman and a black woman in Macon with these words:

> The amalgamation of the races is not only unnatural,
> but is always productive of deplorable results. Our
> daily observation shows us, that the offspring of these
> unnatural connections are generally sickly and effemi-
> nate, and that they are inferior in physical develop-
> ment and strength, to the fullblood of either race.
> . . . There are gradations and classes throughout
> the universe. From the tallest archangel in Heaven,
> down to the meanest reptile on earth, moral and social
> inequalities exist, and must continue to exist through
> all eternity.[28]

Three years later, a Tennessee judge said it was an indict-
able offense for a racially mixed couple who had married legally elsewhere to live together as man and wife in Tennessee. Consider the implications, he wrote:

> . . . we might have in Tennessee the father living
> with his daughter, the son with the mother, the
> brother with his sister, in lawful wedlock, because they
> had formed such relations in a state or country where
> they were not prohibited. The Turk or the Moham-
> medan, with his numerous wives, may establish his harem
> at the doors of the capitol, and we are without remedy.
> Yet none of these are more revolting, more to be
> avoided, or more unnatural than the case before us.[29]

In upholding racial segregation at a municipal golf course eighty years later, a federal judge in Tennessee demonstrated the essential imperturbability of the law. With warnings that "racial differences do not in any way or any degree justify arrogance, pride, intolerance, or abuse," Judge Wilkin used the theory of evolution only lately legalized in Tennessee, the site of the Scopes monkey trial, to arrive at the same conclusion other Southern judges had found in the sentiments of the Bible:

> As nature has produced different species, so it has produced different races of man. Distinguishing racial features have not been produced by man, or man-made laws. They are the result of processes of evolution and it seems natural and customary for different species and different races to recognize and prefer as intimate associates their own kind. Nature has produced white birds, black birds, blue birds, and red birds, and they do not roost on the same limb or use the same nest. Such recognition and preference for their own kind prevails among other animals. It prevails also among all people, among the yellow, black, and red skinned races.[30]

Whether the grand design is according to the laws of nature or of nature's God, to use Jefferson's distinction, it is inexorable. Said Justice Terrell of Florida in 1955:

> . . . segregation is not a new philosophy generated by the states that practice it. It is and always has been the unvarying law of the animal kingdom. The dove and the quail, the turkey and the turkey buzzard, the chicken and the guinea, it matters not where they are found, are segregated; place the horse, the cow, the sheep, the goat and the pig in the same pasture and they instinctively segregate; the fish in the sea segre-

gate into "schools" of their kind; when the goose and
the duck arise from the Canadian marshes and take off
for the Gulf of Mexico and other points in the South
they are always found segregated; and when God created man, he allotted each race his own continent according to color, Europe to the white man, Asia to the
yellow man, Africa to the black man, and America to
the red man, but we are now advised that God's plan
was in error and must be reversed despite the fact that
gregariousness has been the law of the various species
of the animal kingdom.[31]

Even more recently, in the school desegregation case already described, United States District Court Judge T.
Whitfield Davidson, Democrat, Texan, and Episcopalian,
drew together a full body of southern tradition in one grand
obiter dictum. First he establishes his authority to comment
with some sympathy and understanding on questions of
race:

> My grandfather and great-grandfather had many,
> many slaves. My great-grandfather built his slaves
> brick houses that they might be comfortable. He
> taught them to be good carpenters, to be good brick-
> layers as well as farmers. He used a Negro for foreman
> and never let a slave be whipped except upon his own
> orders.[32]

Then he gives his theory of racial cooperation, based on a
segregationist precedent the Supreme Court had repudiated
some years before:

> The formula of Booker Washington for the Negro's
> future was embraced in the word *excellence* and along
> the same line was a former decision of our highest
> court which at the time was the law as it interpreted it,
> rendered in 1896, the case being *Plessy* v. *Ferguson*.

That decision in effect provided that the Negro as a race was entitled under the Constitution to equal opportunities in every field covered by the Constitution and the law of the land. In other words, it embraced the very epitome of free government—equal opportunities. Equal opportunity to the youth is held out in every schoolroom, in every court, in all elements of justice and freedom. Equal opportunity to the black race and the white race has long been the policy of our government.[33]

In the South, says Judge Davidson, the white and black races have progressed side by side, in friendship and understanding.

. . . When [a Negro] puts his hat under his arm and approaches [his] white friend he gets what he came for whether it be a counsellor, an adviser or if need be a champion. . . . The influential white man was his leader and the colored man was the boy or his ward and friend. . . .

The Southern Negro feels kindly to his white neighbor and that feeling is fully reciprocated. Under the guidance and leadership of this influential white neighbor the Southern Negro is freer from wrongdoing than his brethren who have strayed into other fields.[34]

The relevance of racial history to the problem at hand—school integration—is then set out by the judge.

An old sage once remarked that your children will marry whomever they associate with. . . .

This plan of starting with the lower grade and in 12 years completing the integration is in all probability the most direct and surest route to amalgamation which in the long run is the most objectionable of all features of integration.[35]

Racial purity, he feels, is as important for blacks as it is for
whites:

> The Negro has a racial pride where he is let alone as
> well as the white. And he has something to be proud
> of. His advancement from slavery has been one of the
> most marvelous stories ever told. He has a right to
> have his child or his grandchild to be born black like
> he is.
>   . . . An elderly darkie observing a mulatto child:
> "He can't help it. I feel kindly toward him, but I don't
> think much of his mama and papa." [36]

What distinguishes the arguments of Judge Davidson
from those of most of his colleagues on federal and state
benches is not so much their purpose as their ingenuous-
ness. Only in California did judges find an antimiscegenation law unconstitutional, before *Loving* v. *Virginia*.
Many other judges have opposed integration and racial mixture with vigor equal to Davidson's, but have had the wit to
mask their feelings with lawyers' phrases and genteel dissimulation. A parallel is seen in the words and actions of the
executive branch of the national government. In the last few
decades the rhetoric of executive officers has been largely
egalitarian, but the performance of their agencies in support
of civil rights has been erratic. A good example is the behavior of the Federal Bureau of Investigation and its late direc-
tor, J. Edgar Hoover, who apparently placed wiretaps on
the phones of the Reverend Martin Luther King, Jr., partly
as a result of his supposed Communist associations and
partly because of his rumored interracial sexual adventures.
Hoover was cautious in public statements, but reportedly
told a group of newsmen and members of Congress confi-
dentially that King was a "moral degenerate." [37] Always reluctant to commit resources of the FBI to enforcement of
civil rights laws, Hoover may have felt that Martin Luther

King in his public and private life alike was the ultimate affront to American morality and love of country.

Science

Finding little or no support for an attack on antimiscegenation laws in the legal traditions of the country, the Supreme Court might have considered turning to science as a substitute authority. In *Brown* v. *Board of Education* the justices had cited psychological studies of the impact of segregation on black students to bolster their departures from legal tradition. In science and medicine as in law there have been many arguments for and against racial mixing, some learned, some not. Unlike the judges whose writing we have examined, most scientists expounding on race have been egalitarians. Yet even so, the record is so full of contradiction that nonscientists might have trouble choosing sides. Science has therefore been of limited utility.

Let us take some examples. Blood and transfusions have excited the attention of people with strong racial views. In World War I the blood of blacks was turned away by the Red Cross, and later accepted for donation only to black soldiers, in deference to the general fear that it would infect whites with racial disabilities or alien genes transmittable to succeeding generations. As recently as 1943, anthropologist Ashley Montagu took pains to rehearse and dismiss the blood-and-race myths which had enjoyed a revival under Hitler. Montagu assured the readers of *Psychiatry*—who were unlikely to require instruction in the errors of racial prejudice—that blood does not transmit hereditary characters, is not passed from mother to child *in utero*, and is essentially the same for all humans except for properties represented by blood groups. Strange indeed, he thought, that some white people would balk at black blood in a lifesaving

Race, Marriage, and the Law

transfusion and then accept horse serum without question.[38]
A 1944 public opinion poll showed Americans about evenly
divided among those who thought Negro and white blood
the same, different, or did not know which.[39]

On other questions of racial mixture, professional opinion
is divided and increasingly cautious. In the past, doctors of
medicine have joined amateurs in declaring the children of
mixed marriages deficient in one respect or another. The
1896 *Transactions of the American Surgical Association* offers the information that pure-blooded blacks rarely have
dental cavities but that mulattoes frequently do.[40] From the
same period, one learns from the *Journal of the American
Medical Association,* in an article by W. A. Dixon, M.D., of
Ohio, about the "Morbid Proclivities and Retrogressive
Tendencies in the Offspring of Mulattoes," a collection of
casual impressions in the style of science. Dixon had observed the offspring of mulattoes in his border community
for a period of thirty years.

> I can trace some of these families through three or
> four generations. Those of the first cross were robust;
> those of the second were paler, more ashlike in com-
> plexion, of slender form, plainly bearing many of the
> characteristics of predisposition or inevitable tenden-
> cies to special diseases, of the strumous type. The third
> union resulted in less fertility and greater predisposi-
> tion to disease. Now, the children present the scrofu-
> lous physiognomy. The fourth union, still less fertile
> than the others, brings forth a progeny largely suffer-
> ing from cutaneous affections, ophthalmia, rickets,
> dropsy of the head, white swelling of the knee joints,
> morbus coxarius, diseased glands, [and] suppurating
> sores until the whole generation is quite extinct.

Dr. Dixon suggests unconvincingly that the disabilities he
observed are inherited and that none of the mixed-blood's
handicaps stems from discrimination by whites.

These people have had all the advantages that their neighbors enjoyed. . . .

They were able to maintain an academy of learning, from which their sons and daughters could go forth amply equipped to struggle in the unequal contest of life. All of these institutions succumbed to the waning constitutional vigor of their offspring. The academy is no more. . . .

The contrast between the histories of the mulatto and the white and the negro families residing side by side, as to health, as to power to resist disease, and as to longevity, is too great to escape notice, or to be regarded as merely incidental. It is now observable by the colored people themselves that if a mulatto marries back to the parent stock, the children escape to a greater degree scrofulous affections. . . .

Are there any races comparatively free from tuberculosis and all strumous affections? Wherever you see the purity of race maintained, in civilized or barbarous countries, there you see little or no tuberculosis and scrofula. . . .

Dixon closes with a passage from the writing of anthropologist Paul Broca:

the United States, where the Anglo-Saxon race is still predominant, but which is overrun by immigrants of various other races, is by that very circumstance, threatened with decay, inasmuch as this continuous immigration may have the effect of producing a hybrid race containing the germ of disease, decay and future sterility. There are serious men who have predicted from ethnological causes, the overthrow of the United States. . . .[41]

In a euphoric rebuttal some years later, the author of a book entitled *The Melting Pot* contended that, to the contrary,

America would one day have a new blend, a race of super-men endowed with the same hybrid vigor naturalists had discovered in lower forms of life.

The truth is less dramatic than either extreme: there is some modest evidence that the mixing of races may produce offspring who are marginally more fit to survive and repro-duce than their forebears of purer stock. Old studies of the *Bounty* mutineers, white men who married Tahitians and fathered a new crossbreed on Pitcairn Island, of Hottentot-white mixture in Africa, and of the mingling of many strains in Hawaii all suggest that the offspring are as fit as their ancestors, and perhaps fitter. In fact, in the latter two in-stances the offspring exhibited a markedly higher fertility rate than either parent stock, in apparent refutation of the old tale that racially mixed persons are likely to be infertile, on the model of the mule.[42] The horse and the donkey are of different species, but humans of different description are not, so there is no risk of sterility in human crossbreeding. From his review of the scientific literature, Montagu con-cluded that no harmful biological effects of racial mixture have been found, and that in the case of black-white combi-nations there may indeed be some advantage, in a lower in-cidence of congenital malformation.[43] In his opinion, hybrid-ization is broadly beneficial to humans as it is to other species—a statement more of faith than fact, given the state of our knowledge of race. Montagu rejects as a racist canard the suggestion that sickle-cell anemia may be deadlier in mulattoes than in blacks.[44] But N. A. Barnicot posed the sickle-cell problem as an illustration of the possibility of "di-minished fitness" in his balanced essay of the same year. Barnicot, no racist, concluded that, because of the problems of accurate testing, the question of the fitness of human hy-brids could not be answered with any certainty at present and should remain open.[45]

Psychiatrists have entered the fray by attempting to calm

white anxieties about racial mixing. In 1957 some 185 of them, called the Group for the Advancement of Psychiatry, published *Psychiatric Aspects of School Desegregation,* a pamphlet supporting the Supreme Court's efforts to integrate the public schools. In a section on miscegenation, the psychiatrists described some of the causes of racial prejudice in simple language, assured their readers that intermarriage would occur infrequently as long as the matching of personal and social characteristics of prospective partners remained much closer within than between races, and, for those who intermarry, discounted the possibility of "throwbacks," such as black children from the marriage of a white and a mulatto.[46] The Group for the Advancement of Psychiatry, according to its statement of purpose, wished through its publications to bring current professional knowledge to bear on problems of mental health and human relations in the community,[47] a challenge in the case of a discipline as abstruse as psychiatry.

Finally, some lively professional exchanges have been triggered by the publication of *Race and Reason* by nonscientist Carleton Putnam, who contends that miscegenation is undesirable for humanity even if it is a natural propensity. In *Race and Reason* Putnam poses the question, "If the races, left to themselves, tend to intermarry, doesn't this mean that it is the natural thing to do?" and responds, "Consider a garden that has been carefully cultivated for many years. What happens if it is left to nature?" [48]

Very much in the same vein as Sass and Judge Davidson, Putnam asserts that the white southerner loves the Negro, understands him, and has given him every opportunity to perfect himself. The sad reality, according to Putnam, is that the Negro is inferior. He has made few if any contributions to civilization. "We were all in caves or trees originally. The progress which the pure-blooded black has made when left to himself, with a minimum of white help or hindrance, genetically or otherwise, can be measured today in the Congo." [49] To Putnam, all that white culture offers is threatened by miscegenation.

Critics have questioned whether the book is a serious work of anthropology or a political tract written to impede the desegregation of public schools. One of the author's claims to scholarly legitimacy is a laudatory foreword by Messrs. Gates, Garrett, Gayre, and George, who collectively hold an impressive list of academic degrees. Montagu, in a letter to the *New York Times,* again alleging racism in the guise of scientific truth, found their credentials wanting. Gates was no anthropologist, wrote Montagu. He had demonstrated the limits of his expertise by making public remarks about nonexistent Indian wolf children. Garrett was a psychologist and George an anatomist, neither with the understanding of anthropology one needs for intelligent commentary on the questions raised by Putnam, who indeed had himself cited no works of anthropology in *Race and Reason.* And Gayre, he remarked in closing, was a heraldist, for what that might be worth. [50]

Shortly Gayre responded that he had once been a professor of anthropology before turning to heraldry, that Garrett was an *ethno*psychologist, and that Theodosius Dobzhansky, cited by Montagu as a true scientist who recognized Putnam for the propagandist he was, might claim authority on the subject of fruit flies but was scarcely competent to expound on complex matters of race. [51]

One additional round in the battle of credentials must be noted, to show the difficulty of bringing about any meaningful confrontation of science and popular opinion. Another letter to the *Times,* from one Catherine Wepy, gave evidence that the quartet who wrote Putnam's foreword were respectable scientists. They might be right or wrong on problems of race, but they were respectable. George had headed the Anatomy Department at the University of North

Carolina for ten years, she said, and Garrett had been chairman of the Psychology Department at Columbia for fifteen.[52]

The entire exchange advanced public understanding of
race and miscegenation very little. Garrett by this time had
moved from New York City to what may have been the
more congenial setting of the University of Virginia, where
he aired his views on the catastrophe of racial mixing. The
Negro, he said, has less abstract intelligence than the white;
he is less proficient with words, numbers, and symbols. Left
to himself, as he was for a long time in Africa south of the
Sahara, the black man proved unable to develop a literate
civilization, or a bridge or a terrace, or a wheel, or domesti-
cated animals. In all likelihood, thought Garrett, he did not
even have fire. The danger today is that blacks will be
thrown in with whites in school and be tempted futilely to
try amalgamation as the path to equality.[53]

Goaded by the attention paid Garrett, Putnam, George,
and others of their persuasion, the scientific establishment at
last loosed a counterattack, "a response to the barrage of
pseudoscientific statements which, since the Supreme Court
desegregation decision of 1954, have attempted to prove the
innate biological inferiority of the group of Americans who
are socially classified as Negro." [54] A group of geneticists, zo-
ologists, anthropologists, and psychiatrists under the direction of Margaret Mead and Theodosius Dobzhansky
organized a symposium on the biological, social, and
psychological aspects of race in man, held during the meet-
ings of the American Association for the Advancement of
Science in Washington, D. C., in December 1966. Papers
were presented on "The Need to End the Pseudoscientific
Investigation of Race," "Racial Classifications: Popular and
Scientific," and other topics, along with the separate view of
Dwight Ingle, chairman of the Department of Physiology at
the University of Chicago, that the equality of races is un-

proven and that there ought to be investigations of average
biological differences among racial groups rather than a
general avoidance of serious research.[55] Little fresh research
on racial differences had been published in the preceding
thirty years, Mead agreed, because of the perversion of race
theory under the Nazis and a feeling among reputable scientists that it might be prudent to ignore the subject altogether. But what research there was indicated "the comparable capacities of all large-sized human populations." She and
others criticized the method Montagu had used to reach the
same conclusion: he believed there was no shred of
evidence that mental ability and cultural achievement are
related to genes linked with those for physical characteristics—and if there are differences, they are minute—but
denied the existence of anything properly called "race"
among humans.[56]

Even with the publication of the papers and discussions
of the symposium months later, the views which gained the
widest circulation and affected public opinion the most
were those of the publicists representing the polar positions,
Putnam and Montagu.

The issue of the genetic inequality of human races was re-
vived for a time by the publication of "How Much Can We
Boost IQ and Scholastic Achievement?" by Arthur Jensen
in the Winter 1969 *Harvard Educational Review*. This article attributed some 80 percent of the difference between average black and white intelligence scores to genes, and it
occasioned an outbreak of rejoinders in the newspapers and
journals. But by 1971 there were signs of growing indifference to the question. In April the National Academy of
Sciences, after listening to the report of a committee on the
study of racial differences, rejected motions to support further investigation in such directions as the educational implications of human behavioral genetics and the interaction
of genetic and environmental factors in human perfor-

mance.[57] The members of the academy preferred not to commit more forces to an unwinnable war.

Extracts from the scientific literature might reinforce the Court's willingness to remove the last vestiges of racial discrimination from the law books of the states, but the states could play at the same game, with dubious proofs of racial difference or the more learned argument that exact measures of racial equality or the effects of mixing are not yet available. The scientific community did offer the Court more support than public opinion or case law for an attack on antimiscegenation statutes. Still, the clearest support of all had to come from another source: churches.

Religion

Religious groups had been especially indignant about the offending laws. The national conference of the United Presbyterian Church condemned the "blasphemy and neurosis of racism" in 1965, and overwhelmingly approved a resolution asserting the absence of theological grounds for opposition to interracial marriage and the duty of church members to work for the repeal of antimiscegenation laws.[58] According to a position paper of the conference, racism

considers it regrettable, but tolerable, that two mismatched persons of the same race are permitted to marry, but can think of no way legally to prohibit such a marriage without depriving the subjects of their human and constitutional rights. Yet the same racism finds the most tenuous rationalizations for state laws that prohibit "miscegenation" and sees no violations of human or constitutional right in such laws. And where no laws exist, white custom and prejudice decree social punishment for those who dare to break with custom.[59]

The new moderator of the United Presbyterian conference expressed the conviction that miscegenation statutes "deny basic human rights," but added that mixed marriages do "bring all kinds of tensions within the family" and therefore he "ought not to be understood as encouraging them." [60] A year later the International Convention of the Disciples of Christ passed a resolution, after agonizing debate, calling on Disciples to "overcome" racial marriage laws. Dissenters to the resolution felt that more education might be needed before the freedom to intermarry would be meaningful, or that it might be prudent not to put other civil rights in jeopardy by raising the delicate issue of racial intermarriage. [61]

Acting on principle, not prejudice or considerations of strategy, these church groups and others could speak in simple, unequivocal moral terms of the freedom to marry. Public opinion polls indicated that a majority of well-educated American adults agreed with church moralists on the undesirability of antimiscegenation laws. In reaching a conclusion approved by this minority and disapproved by the general public, though, the Supreme Court would do only what it had often done before: polls tend to show the unpopularity both of the Court's decisions asserting the rights of individuals and of the underlying constitutional provisions. Only a minority, with higher education, favors the principles of the Constitution. [62] If the Bill of Rights or the Fourteenth Amendment were put before the voters in a referendum, it would be defeated. It is no wonder that the Supreme Court does not slavishly follow public opinion. It may fear the public and the perennial threat of congressional retaliation for an unpopular ruling, and it may time and trim its decisions to minimize criticism, but it cannot in good conscience reflect popular views of the rights of man.

That the climate of opinion for its decision on state antimiscegenation laws was one of prejudice and hostility relieved only by the support of a tolerant few was not, therefore, an unusual predicament for the Court. The question for the Court was not whether its ruling would be popular, but whether its unpopularity would be down to a safe level by mid-1967.

Miscegenation and the Law Before 1967

Antimiscegenation laws

Richard and Mildred Loving defied an old tradition in their state. Virginia's antimiscegenation laws dated from 1691, though the first recorded in the New World was Maryland's thirty years earlier. In the following two hundred years many of the American colonies and states of the union passed such statutes, invariably directed at black-white mixing and often other combinations as well: Malayans, American Indians, Chinese, Koreans, Japanese, Ethiopians, Hindus, and so forth. Thirty-eight of the states had antimiscegenation laws at one time or another.[1] During the years of the Civil War the number of laws dwindled, except in the South where they remained intact. By the end of the Second World War, thirty-one states had such statutes. By the year of the *Loving* case, fifteen of these had repealed or voided their laws.[2] The remaining states were Alabama, Arkansas, Delaware, Florida, Georgia, Kentucky, Louisiana, Mississippi, Missouri, North Carolina, Oklahoma, South Carolina, Tennessee, Texas, Virginia, and West Virginia.

The avowed purpose of Virginia's law of 1691 was the prevention of "abominable mixture and spurious issue." The same act required any white Englishwoman who had a child by a Negro to pay fifteen pounds to the church wardens or, if she failed to do that, to become an indentured

servant for five years. The child in any event would be
bound out by the wardens for a period of thirty years. The
miscegenation provisions were tightened by amendments
in 1924, which narrowed the definition of "white persons" to
"no trace whatever" of nonwhite blood and for the first time
in Virginia prohibited white marriage with orientals and
other nonwhite non-Negroes.[3] (Some critics were disposed
to wonder what the legal effect of a transfusion of black
blood into white veins would be. Louisiana had attempted
to meet the problem by requiring that a white patient be
notified specifically if a black man's blood were all that
could be found for transfusion and that he be given an opportunity to refuse it.)

> Virginia Code § 1–14.: Colored persons and Indians
> defined.—Every person in whom there is ascertainable
> any Negro blood shall be deemed and taken to be a
> colored person, and every person not a colored person
> having one-fourth or more of American Indian blood
> shall be deemed an American Indian; except that mem-
> bers of Indian tribes existing in this Commonwealth
> having one-fourth or more of Indian blood and less
> than one-sixteenth of Negro blood shall be deemed
> tribal Indians.

> Virginia Code § 20–54.: Intermarriage prohibited;
> meaning of term "white persons."—It shall hereafter be
> unlawful for any white person in this State to marry
> any save a white person, or a person with no other ad-
> mixture of blood than white and American Indian. For
> the purpose of this chapter, the term "white person"
> shall apply only to such person as has no trace what-
> ever of any blood other than Caucasian; but persons
> who have one-sixteenth or less of the blood of the
> American Indian and have no other non-Caucasian
> blood shall be deemed to be white persons. All laws

heretofore passed and now in effect regarding the intermarriage of white and colored persons shall apply to
marriages prohibited by this chapter.[4]

The difference between the "no trace whatever" of black
blood allowable in a "white" person and the one-sixteenth
Indian blood permitted is due to a combination of custom
and historical tradition in Virginia. It is customary throughout the country for a person with any detectable negroid
features or color to be called Negro. But Virginia has as a
chapter in its proud history the marriage of a white settler,
John Rolfe, and an Indian princess, Pocahontas. The one-
sixteenth provision was an exemption from the no-trace
rule, enacted to protect the legitimacy of the descendants of
Rolfe and Pocahontas, though it would not have allowed the
marriage itself or even legitimized the first generations of
children of the two. Mildred Loving had Indian ancestors
and Negro both, but the arithmetic of blood was of no concern in this case because of an understanding among the
parties at each stage of the litigation that she was and was
to be considered a Negro.

The Virginia law went on to fix penalties.

> Virginia Code § 20–59.: Punishment for marriage.—If
> any white person intermarry with a colored person, or
> any colored person intermarry with a white person, he
> shall be guilty of a felony and shall be punished by
> confinement in the penitentiary for not less than one
> nor more than five years.

The Lovings were tried and convicted under a companion
section designed to fill an obvious loophole in § 20–59.

> Virginia Code § 20–58.: Leaving State to evade
> law.—If any white person and colored person shall
> go out of this State, for the purpose of being

married, and the intention of returning, and be
married out of it, and afterwards return to and
reside in it, cohabiting as man and wife, they
shall be punished as provided in § 20–59, and the
marriage shall be governed by the same law as if
it had been solemnized in this State. The fact
of their cohabitation here as man and wife shall
be evidence of their marriage.[5]

The 1924 act was originally entitled "A bill to preserve
the integrity of the white race," although as we shall see, it
was later defended on more generally acceptable grounds.
Earnest Sevier Cox, in a book called *The South's Part in
Mongrelizing the Nation*, published in Richmond in 1926,
called the 1924 act "probably the most perfected expression
of the white racial ideal since the institution of caste in
India some four thousand years ago." [6] In the city of Richmond, the mixed marriage law was reinforced by a roundabout ordinance prohibiting the use of a residence by any
person who would be disqualified for marriage into a majority of the families already on the block.[7]

Antimiscegenation laws have not prevented racial mixture
in the United States, it goes without saying. An estimated
three-fourths to four-fifths of the American Negro population has some white ancestry. Very little of the mixing has
come about by intermarriage. Most children of mixed parentage would have been illegitimate with or without the
laws, the offspring of white men and black women. Until
the Supreme Court ruled against them in 1964, a number of
states attached harsher penalties to interracial sexual relations or cohabitation than to the same conduct by members
of one race. But these provisions too, while more relevant to
the pervasive mixture of the races in the United States, have
been largely unenforced, if not unenforceable.

Enforcement of the laws

Occasional reports in the newspapers of the enforcement of antimiscegenation laws give us a hint of the suffering that occurs when race laws destroy a marriage. Davis K—— of Ellisville, Mississippi, was sentenced to five years in jail in 1949 for his marriage to a white girl, although he had lived his life as a white in the white part of town and came from a family that had been considered white for the seventy years that older residents of Ellisville could recall. He had no negroid features. But rumors had circulated, and trial and conviction followed. K——'s last futile defense was that if indeed he had a trace of nonwhite blood it must have been American Indian, not Negro.[8]

In the same year, a young man was brought to trial in Roanoke, Virginia, because his mother-in-law one night had a dream in which he appeared black rather than his customary white. Clark H—— had visited his girl's family often while he was stationed at a nearby naval base, and had been well received. The wedding was performed by a Baptist minister who later said, "He seemed to be a white man. . . . He seemed to be very genteel and nice and I invited them to join my Bible class if they settled in Roanoke." Then relations cooled. The father of the bride afterwards recalled that "he seemed to be getting darker after they were married," and then within weeks came the dream and the arrest. There was some question whether H—— should be held for trial in the white or the colored part of jail pending possible reclassification. According to the sheriff's deputy who made the difficult decision, he was "not too dark— perhaps a little yellow, with brown hair, a little bit curly"— one who could pass as an "average white man." So he placed H—— in a cell for whites. The bride was thought to be of the honest opinion that H—— was white, and was not prosecuted.[9]

In Louisiana a college basketball star went to the county courthouse for a license to marry the daughter of a prominent white family and discovered that he was a Negro because of a black ancestor on record. The girl's family was reported to be upset. The couple chose to avoid a dispute with law or family, left for California, married, and have not been heard from again.[10]

Sometimes couples were prosecuted for miscegenation involving neither marriage nor cohabitation. An appellate court in Alabama upheld the conviction of a white woman, Luby G——, for "adultery or fornication" with a black man "against the peace and dignity of the State of Alabama." Consider the intrusiveness of the community's interest in the private lives of its citizens, as described by Judge Price:

> Appellant, a white woman, was indicted jointly with Nathan B——, a Negro man, on a charge of miscegenation. . . . The trial resulted in the conviction of the defendant and the court sentenced her to imprisonment in the penitentiary for seven years. From the judgment of conviction this appeal was taken.
>
> The State's contention is as follows: Appellant and her husband operated a store in a Negro community. Nathan B—— was seen frequently in and around the store. Appellant and the said B—— were seen riding together many times in appellant's automobile. They would drive away from the store, remain gone for awhile and then return. They were also seen hugging and kissing in the back of the store.
>
> One afternoon appellant found Nathan at the home of Miley M——, a Negro woman. A short time afterward she returned to Miley's house and told her that she, appellant, had been going with Nathan for four

years and if she ever caught Miley and Nathan together she would kill them. . . .

Still more damning evidence of the wrongdoings of the two
was adduced:

> Appellant and Nathan were seen near a creek by
> Elmo G——, a cousin of appellant's husband. They
> were behind a bank of dirt and Nathan ran away.
> On one occasion appellant left a box and sack con-
> taining a lunch and whiskey and Coca Cola for Nathan
> at the home of Willie Mae W——, a colored woman.
> Nathan was working at a nearby sawmill and he came
> in at noon and ate the food and drank the whiskey.
> They were seen together on an abandoned sawmill
> road. Appellant was sitting in her car with the door
> open and Nathan was standing by the open door. Ap-
> pellant told the colored man who saw them not to tell
> anybody and "not to have anything to do with white
> folks' business." About four weeks later this witness
> was in appellant's store and she told him again not to
> tell what he had seen. This witness later saw Nathan
> go in the back door of appellant's house at night when
> her husband was away and he watched for more than
> an hour and Nathan did not reappear.
> Another colored man saw Luby G—— go into the
> woods on several occasions, followed shortly thereafter
> by Nathan B——. Appellant told witness not to tell
> anybody what he had seen and gave him two shirts.
> All of the State's evidence was denied by defendant.
> She insisted she never had sexual intercourse with Na-
> than B——. She stated that she or her husband often
> drove negro customers home when they had bought
> groceries too heavy to carry. She testified she had done
> sewing for colored people and had quarreled with

Miley M—— over the price of sewing and whiskey her husband had bought from Miley.

After this long recital of evidence in the case, the judge gave his decision:

> It has been stated many times that to make out a case of miscegenation or living in adultery, it is not necessary for the State to introduce positive evidence of an act of intercourse. These are offenses which can rarely be directly proved, but must in the great majority of cases be inferred from a chain of circumstances. There was sufficient evidence to justify the court in submitting the case to the jury.
>
> The motion for a new trial was properly refused. . . . Affirmed.[11]

Punishment for miscegenation in the statutes still in force in the 1960s was thirty days or one hundred dollars in Delaware, and up to a maximum of ten years in jail in Florida, Indiana, Maryland, Mississippi, and North Carolina.[12] Definitions of "colored" or "Negro" varied among the states. For example, at one time one was a Negro in Georgia if he had one Negro great-great-grandparent, but was white in adjacent Florida, which set its line of distinction at one black great-grandparent.[13] Within these states it sometimes happened that definitions differed according to circumstance—a person with fractional black ancestry could qualify for attendance at a white public school but be unsuited for marriage to a white later on. There were still other oddities. In 1962 Pvt. Paul F—— of North Carolina, stationed with the Army in South Carolina, tried and failed to obtain a license to marry Lorena S——, an Indian from North Carolina. State law permitted whites to marry Catawba Indians, but she was a Cherokee.[14] Alabama forbade marriage of a white man with anyone with Negro ancestry, but pun-

ished only when a white married someone with one-eighth or
more black admixture.[15] Proof was often difficult. Said
one court, "It was proper to prove that defendant's grandfa-
ther had 'kinky hair.'" [16]

Some states prohibited intermarriage but not sexual relations, as Mississippians discovered one day in 1958 when the
conviction of Daisey R——, black female, and Elsie A——,
white male, for interracial cohabitation was thrown out by
an appellate judge on the ground that a close reading of the
law indicated that it did not in fact apply to relations outside of marriage.[17] Mississippians felt strongly enough to
make publication of "general information, arguments or
suggestions in favor of social equality or intermarriage between whites and Negroes" a crime.[18] Arizona once had a
law so involved it made marriage of a mulatto to anyone,
even another mulatto, unlawful. The law did to him what
nature had done to the mule. But the law was repaired. The
mulatto was given a measure of relief: he could marry an
Indian, but he was still forbidden to marry a Negro, a Caucasian, or another mulatto.[19]

To circumvent the restrictions of state law, would-be miscegenationists were sometimes tempted to marry out of
state with the hope of returning later in peace. But the general rule was that entry or re-entry afforded no advantage.
Virginia law as it applied to the Lovings was typical, speci-
fying penalties for fixed and moving miscegenation alike.
California's statutes, which were overturned by its high
court in 1948, were at the other extreme, prohibiting interracial marriages but attaching no criminal penalties to such
marriages, to attempted interracial marriage, to interracial
cohabitation, or to migration into California by miscegenous
couples legally wed elsewhere.[20] (About the only limit to
California's generous recognition of out-of-state marriages
was handed down in 1898 in a nonracial case involving two

young people who attempted to evade the hardships of a
law forbidding the marriage of fifteen-year-olds without parental consent by hiring the schooner *Willy* and the services
of its captain for a ceremony nine miles out to sea and a
triumphal return to Los Angeles as man and wife. The court
said no.) [21]

In the less forgiving South, those who were determined to
marry across race lines had to choose between a secret relationship or flight north. The most celebrated of these
unions, seen equally by integrationists as evidence of the inhu-
manity of white southern mores and by segregationists as
proof of the dangers of school integration, was the secret
marriage of Charlayne H—— and Walter S—— in the North
in March 1963. They returned to the South to continue their
studies at the University of Georgia, where Miss H—— had
been one of two Negroes to break the color bar with the aid
of a court order two years before. When their secret was revealed in the fall, University of Georgia President O. C. Ad-
erhold confessed feeling "greatly surprised and shocked." He
said, "Interracial marriage is prohibited by Georgia law and
secret marriages are contrary to University of Georgia regulations. Dismissal rules would have applied to Charlayne H
—— and Walter S—— had the fact of their secret marriage
been known. Neither, therefore, will be permitted to return
to the University of Georgia." [22] Once again out of the state,
with plans to settle in New York, the couple was threatened
by Georgia Attorney General Eugene Cook with prosecution if they ever returned.[23] Scarcely less unrelenting was
the reaction of S——'s father, a prominent Georgian manu-
facturer of chicken feed, who told newsmen, "This is the
end of the world." [24] Walter S—— had returned to the university after serving with the army in Europe. He met Miss
H—— in a coffee shop on campus in 1962. "There was only
one seat—across from Charlayne—and I sat there." [25] They

met discreetly on campus and off during the months that
followed until their marriage and what they described as
"our honeymoon on the turnpike" in the spring.[26]

Arthur Krock of the *New York Times* commented that
miscegenation was

> the principal reason for the last-ditch white Southern
> resistance to the proposed Federal laws which forbid
> compulsory segregation in schools and wherever else
> the two races would come together in more or less inti-
> mate contact. . . .
>
> This reason has gone largely unpublicized in the rec-
> ords of the Southern resistance, including restraining
> actions in the state and Federal courts. But the reac-
> tions in the South to the Georgia mixed marriage have
> brought this factor violently to the surface. . . .[27]

For some couples, the only asylum was a border crossing.
Missouri prohibited the marriage of Diane G——, white,
with Benjamin A——, whose part-Filipino ancestry made
him a Mongolian in the eyes of St. Louis authorities. They
were married on the other side of the Mississippi in Illinois,
where there were no rules against Mongolian-white marriages.[28] When Meki T——, a singer and dancer from
Samoa, and his Caucasian fiancée from Baltimore were refused a license in Maryland in 1966, their departure for the
District of Columbia and wedding there were covered in
detail by the news media. Readers learned that Maryland
race law had been amended in 1935 to prohibit the marriage of the "brown" or "Malay" race to whites in order to
discourage Filipino mess boys at the United States Naval
Academy from taking local brides. The statute allowed a
brown or white person to marry anyone who was red or yellow, but forbade white-brown unions along with white-
black. Senator Daniel Inouye of Hawaii protested that Maryland law would find half of the people of his state

impure.[29] In 1964 Maryland Judge Albert Menchine had ordered a recalcitrant clerk to issue a license to a Filipino
physician and his white fiancée, but he left the statute intact. Judge Menchine avoided a constitutional ruling by
finding that the doctor had a white grandmother. "Assum-
ing that in general a Filipino is a member of the Malay race,
it is very clear that this Filipino is not," he said.[30] The next
year a bad guess about the impact of this case was recorded
in the pages of the *Maryland Law Review:* "The holding
. . . indicates that the Maryland miscegenation statute, because of its doubtful constitutionality, is unlikely to be
enforced." [31]

For several weeks after the T—— incident, Negro legislators in Maryland tried to expunge the state's race laws. The
Maryland senate refused by a vote of fifteen to thirteen,
then reversed itself sixteen to eleven, only to have the lower
house reject the repeal measure by a small margin.[32] Black
legislator Ernest Young called the laws "an insult" and
white legislator C. Maurice Weidemeyer complained in return that those who favored repeal "want to make this country a brown race." [33] The following year under the leadership of Governor Spiro Agnew, a reapportioned legislature
accomplished the repeal with ease, only weeks before *Loving* v. *Virginia.* One of the casualties of the legislature's action was a venerable provision which a Baltimore judge had
considered unconstitutional a decade before:

> Any white woman who shall suffer or permit herself
> to be got with child by a negro or mulatto, upon con-
> viction thereof in the criminal jurisdiction, either in
> the city or county where such child was begotten or
> where the same child was born, shall be sentenced to
> the penitentiary for not less than eighteen months nor
> more than five years.[34]

Loving v. *Virginia*

It fell to Virginia and to the Lovings to carry the issue of
racial mixture to its conclusion for the nation. Richard and
Mildred Loving were prepared by long experience to question the morality, even the sanity, of Virginia's race laws.
They were born in Caroline County and knew one another
as children. In Central Point, the section of the county
where Richard Loving spent all of his early years, race lines
are less distinct than in most parts of Virginia or the rest of
the South. Central Point, which has been called "the passing
capital of America," has a good many Negro residents who
are sufficiently light-skinned to be taken for white, and relations between races are relaxed there. Richard Loving's father drove a truck for a prosperous Negro farmer for nearly
a quarter of a century, and Richard Loving, a brick mason
with a consuming interest in hot-rod cars, for years was in a
drag-racing partnership with a Negro. Said one resident of
the area, "We've done more integrating than any other part
of the United States." [35]

Some of the Negroes in Central Point "passed" on trips
outside town, going to nearby segregated theaters and restaurants as whites; others incurred the greater risk of marrying as white. It is said that when white relatives visit Central Point, children stay home rather than disclose the
family's race by attending a school or boarding a school bus
that would identify them as black. The Lovings might have
joined the genial conspiracy. As a cousin of Mildred Loving
said, "Richard isn't the first white person in our family." But
they preferred to move into the open.[36]

They decided to marry, knowing Virginia law forbade
their marriage—it levied a fine of two hundred dollars for
the performance of an interracial marriage ceremony as

well, "of which the informer shall have one-half." The District of Columbia, some seventy-five miles to the north and considerably less racist in tone and custom than Virginia, was a place to marry with neither legal impediment nor undue embarrassment. The Lovings were aware that Virginia law also forbade their living as man and wife, no matter where or if a ceremony had been performed, and specifically prohibited racial intermarriage outside the state with intent to return to live. Nevertheless they were married in Washington, D. C., on June 2, 1958, and returned to Caroline County shortly afterward.

On July 11, 1958, less than six weeks after their marriage, arrest warrants were issued by Justice of the Peace Robert Farmer "to the sheriff or any police officer" of the county on the complaint of the county prosecutor, Bernard Mahon. According to Mahon, the Lovings had feloniously gone from the state on June 2 with the purpose of marrying and returning. The warrant was "to apprehend and bring before the Judge of said County the body of said Richard Loving to answer the said complaint, and to be further dealt with according to law." An identical warrant was issued for Mildred Loving, though in it and all subsequent legal references to her in Virginia, the state referred to her by her maiden name in order not to bestow any semblance of recognition on the marriage.[37]

On July 13, Richard Loving's warrant of arrest was executed by a visit from Sheriff Garnett Brooks; Mildred "Jeter's" was executed on July 17. The next step was for each to post one thousand dollars bond or its equivalent to assure their appearance in the county court to answer charges. Before Justice of the Peace Edward Stehl, III, on July 17 for Richard Loving and on October 13 for Mildred Loving, each entered a plea of not guilty and was formally answered by Judge Stehl as follows: "Upon the defendant's plea of not guilty to the within charge, and upon examination of the witnesses I find probable cause to charge the accused with a felony and it is ordered that he be held for action of the grand jury."

When the grand jury convened later in the year, it brought formal charges—an indictment or "true bill"—as announced by the foreman Gladys Livermon. The next step was the trial itself before the Caroline County Court of Judge Leon M. Bazile. With the consent of the judge and the prosecutor, the Lovings waived jury trial because the factual issues were fairly simple, because a jury would not be expected to act with much sympathy, and with a judge alone acting with less emotion than a jury there was hope that the laws would be construed to allow the Lovings to continue living in Virginia. After the court heard the evidence and the arguments of the lawyers, the Lovings were induced to change their pleas to guilty. On January 6, 1959, the judge sentenced each to a year in jail, but suspended execution of the sentence on the condition that they leave Virginia and not return together or even at the same time for a period of twenty-five years. Judge Bazile asked the Lovings if either had anything to say before final imposition of the sentence. They did not. The sentence was imposed, and the Lovings paid court costs and were released from custody. They returned to the District of Columbia for the time being.

In 1963 the Lovings wrote to the Attorney General of the United States, Robert F. Kennedy, asking for his help. Kennedy was sympathetic, but he felt there was nothing to be done by his office. He did make a crucial move, however: he referred the Lovings' letter to the American Civil Liberties Union, which appointed two Alexandria, Virginia, attorneys, Bernard Cohen and Philip Hirschkop, to represent them. Cohen and Hirschkop's strategy in contesting the antimiscegenation prosecution was to seek reversal of the verdict in both Virginia and federal courts, understanding that chances would be better in the latter. The Virginia Supreme Court of Appeals was still wont to refer to persons of mixed ancestry as "a mongrel breed." By taking advantage of the federal division of powers, which allows either level of court to strike down a state law as contrary to the national Constitution, the ACLU lawyers at times had cases pending in both courts at once.

In the Virginia courts, their first move was to ask the trial court to reconsider. Cohen and Hirschkop filed a "motion to vacate judgment and set aside sentence," alleging that the Lovings had complied with the conditions of the 1959 sentence but that the laws were unconstitutional and the sentences invalid. In accordance with legal custom, the lawyers advanced every constitutional argument that had even the slimmest chance of moving the trial judge, or the appellate judge after: the punishment was "cruel and unusual," they said, the Lovings had suffered punishment in violation of the due process clause, the Virginia law was a violation of the guarantee of equal protection of the laws, and it was a burden on interstate commerce.

Judge Bazile denied the motion on December 22, 1965. He disposed of the cruel and unusual punishment argument by citing old cases applying that guarantee to the rack, drawing and quartering, leaving the condemned to perish in chains, breaking on the wheel, burning at the stake, and crucifixion, but not to anything as mild as his decree in the trial of the Lovings. He denied that marriage had anything to do with interstate commerce. "There is nothing more domestic than marriage." "If the Federal Government can determine who may marry in a State," he continued, quoting from an opinion of a court in Indiana, a state with a tradition of hostility to the national government paralleling Virginia's, "there is no limit to its power."

To make it clear that he regarded enforcement of the antimiscegenation laws as a moral as well as a legal duty, Judge Bazile concluded reverently:

> Almighty God created the races white, black, yellow, malay, and red, and he placed them on separate continents. And but for the interference with his arrangement there would be no cause for such marriages. The fact that he separated the races shows that he did not intend for the races to mix. . . .
>
> Conviction of a felony is a serious matter. You lose your political rights; and only the government has the power to restore them. And as long as you live you will be known as a felon.
>
> The moving finger writes and moves on
> and having writ
> Nor all your piety nor all your wit
> Can change one line of it.

The stage was now set for appeal in Richmond to Virginia's highest court.

Meanwhile, as the trial court completed its unhurried reconsideration, the ACLU attorneys had filed suit in the United States District Court for the Eastern District of Virginia, asking that a special three-judge panel be convened for the purpose of deciding the constitutionality of Virginia's antimiscegenation laws and enjoining their enforcement by the state. The special panel is a means of obtaining a more authoritative decision or speeding a dispute to the Supreme Court for final dispensation.

The federal court, consisting of Judges Bryson, Butzner, and Lewis, heard arguments by counsel for the Lovings and the State of Virginia on December 28, 1964. The ACLU brief revealed that the Lovings and their three children had returned from Washington, D. C., to Caroline County after the filing of the suit, and that one of the children was at-

tending school in Virginia. The Lovings' counsel had
worked out an agreement with the prosecutor to suspend
further enforcement of the original court order while appeals were pending.

On February 11 the federal court handed down its decision, declining to rule on the Virginia law as long as there
remained a possibility of resolving the issue in a state court.
The ACLU attorneys had argued that the Supreme Court of
Appeals of Virginia had already on several occasions made
its position on miscegenation known and that asking for another opinion would be a waste of time. But the federal
court did maintain an interest in the case, saying that the
threat of imprisonment hanging over the Lovings entitled
them to an answer without delay: either a state court or,
failing that, a federal court would have to rule on their
rights. The three judges were set to take up the case once
more if the state judiciary tried to evade the issue.

Having lost a skirmish, the Lovings' counsel gave the
clerk of the Caroline County Court notice of appeal to the
Virginia Supreme Court of Appeals, "assigning errors" or
points in the interpretation of the law by the trial court
which they hoped to overturn. There was no dispute over
the racial classification of the Lovings or over the fact that
they had violated the Virginia Code. Counsel asserted that
the trial court had erred in not finding the statutes in violation of the equal protection and due process clauses of Section 1 of the Virginia Constitution and the Fourteenth
Amendment of the United States Constitution. They also
contended that the sentence itself was a denial of due process of law. All the questions were ones of constitutionality.
As expected, the Virginia high court sustained the antimiscegenation laws. In an opinion by Judge Carrico the court
found no violation of the equal protection or due process
clauses of the Constitution, although it did modify the sentence to allow the Lovings to return to Virginia together for

visits if they did not "cohabit." It also found fault with
Judge Bazile's original sentence of one year in "jail" for each
of the Lovings because the statute specified "penitentiary."
It did not agree that prohibiting cohabitation within the
state was the equivalent of banishment—the court suggested
the wrongdoers might be "rehabilitated" under their revised
sentence, apparently by being allowed to return to Virginia
and there to behave properly, living apart and contemplating the error of their ways in going against God, nature, and
the traditions of the Commonwealth.

The court relied heavily on the case of *Naim* v. *Naim,* in
which they earlier had upheld the same antimiscegenation
laws. The United States Supreme Court had refused to intervene then. To the works of sociology, biology, and anthropology cited by the ACLU attorneys to counter the
logic of their *Naim* decision, the Virginia court said:

> A decision in this court reversing the *Naim* case
> upon consideration of the opinions of such text writers
> would be judicial legislation in the rawest sense of that
> term. Such arguments are properly addressable to the
> legislature, which enacted the law in the first place,
> and not to this court, whose prescribed role in the sep-
> arated powers of government is to adjudicate and not
> to legislate.

The ACLU's point was that proper adjudication, as they
conceived it, required the court to prefer the mandate of the
Constitution to the provisions of state law, under the established rule that the federal Constitution is supreme. The
next move was to make the same claim in what it hoped
would be a more sympathetic forum, the Supreme Court of
the United States.

Attorneys Cohen and Hirschkop filed notice of appeal to
the United States Supreme Court on May 31, 1966. As be-

fore they proposed a broad array of questions about the legitimacy of the Virginia laws, including consistency with (1) the due process and equal protection clauses, (2) constitutional guarantees of privacy, (3) the constitutional freedom to marry, and (4) civil rights guaranteed by Act of Congress. The references to the rights of privacy and the freedom to marry were designed to make the most of recent speculative statements of the Supreme Court in connection with birth control litigation.

When a case is to be taken "on appeal" to the Supreme Court from a state court, and not by the more usual writ of certiorari, the would-be appellants must convince the Court first of all that a "substantial federal question" is involved. The question or questions may be constitutional or statutory or both. In this preliminary round the parties may test most of their arguments rather than save them for the final confrontation. Arguments were presented in writing by Melvin Wulf and David Carliner for the ACLU and by Attorney General Button of Virginia opposing the Supreme Court's involvement in the case. Wulf and Carliner urged that the effects of the antimiscegenation laws were more pervasive than people generally realized—many rights and benefits were contingent upon the marital relationship. Because of the laws some individuals could not establish a family abode; some children had the stigma of bastardy; the adults were prejudiced with respect to certain tax, social security, insurance, and workmen's compensation benefits; and finally some criminal defenses were not available to them, such as marrying out of a charge of statutory rape, if persons of different races were involved.

Virginia Attorney General Button, in arguing against assumption of jurisdiction by the Supreme Court, employed a combination of historical, legal, and sociological information. First he cited the debate on the Civil Rights Act of 1866 as evidence of congressional intent in proposing the

Fourteenth Amendment for ratification shortly after. For example, this narrow construction:

> But, says the Senator from Indiana, we have laws in Indiana prohibiting black people from marrying whites, and you are trying to disregard these laws? Are our laws enacted for the purpose of preventing amalgamation to be disregarded, and is a man to be punished because he undertakes to enforce them? I beg the Senator from Indiana to read the bill. One of its objects is to secure the same civil rights and subject to the same punishment persons of all races and colors. How does this interfere with the law of Indiana preventing marriages between whites and blacks? Are not both races treated alike by the law of Indiana? Does not the law make it just as much a crime for a white man to marry a black woman as for a black woman to marry a white man, and *vice versa*? I presume there is no discrimination in this respect, and therefore your law forbidding marriage between whites and blacks operates alike on both races. This bill does not interfere with it.

Whether this was historically accurate, and if so whether it was relevant to twentieth century society, was for the Supreme Court to judge.

Next Button pointed to the ostensibly scientific material presented by a dissenting judge in a California case, which tended to support the wisdom of Virginia's laws, but rather than discuss the merits of the scientific controversy Button merely warned the Court that it might become "mired in a veritable Serbonian bog of conflicting scientific opinion on the effects of interracial marriage. . . ." The only work Button quoted was Albert Gordon's *Intermarriage: Interfaith, Interracial, Interethnic,* the standard though tendentious treatise published in 1964. Gordon writes of the children of interracial marriage as "victims," and of intermarriage of all

three kinds as "definitely inadvisable" for the individuals involved and a "threat to society." According to Gordon, not
all who oppose intermarriage are prejudiced—"in fact, to assume so is itself a prejudice." Again, the separate questions
of the validity and relevance of all this information would
be up to the Supreme Court to assess.

The Court's response was to accept the case for review—it
noted probable jurisdiction on December 12, 1966. The next
steps were to be the submission of written briefs and oral argument before the Court on the day appointed. In this final
assault the ACLU was joined by a number of other organizations interested in minority rights, whose combined forces
by now overshadowed the Lovings and their marital travails
—in fact the presence of the Lovings and even knowledge of
the details of their predicament were unnecessary for the
lawyers, who were preparing to argue matters of legal principle and public policy.

Appearing on behalf of Virginia before the Supreme
Court was the State of North Carolina. The American Civil
Liberties Union, various Catholic organizations acting together, the Japanese American Citizens League, the National Association for the Advancement of Colored People,
and the NAACP Legal Defense and Educational Fund came
to the assistance of the Lovings.

In general there are two ways an interest group can affect
Supreme Court decisions directly and openly: by bringing
test cases and by intervening as a friend of the court—
amicus curiae—once a case has arrived. The ACLU acts in
either capacity according to opportunity and the availability
of resources. Finding and grooming a test case is a difficult
process, full of pitfalls. The dispute must be kept alive during the time from trial to final review, often several years. In
one famous case the Supreme Court avoided an embarrassing
review of public school prayer by noting that the pupil in
question had graduated during this period. Equally impor-

tant, the issues that matter to the interest group must be
kept pure. In its public school desegregation strategy, for
example, the NAACP had to find at least one school district
in which the separate facilities for whites and blacks were
indeed equal, apart from their separateness, in order not to
have the case decided according to the separate-but-equal
doctrine of *Plessy* v. *Ferguson,* "Reversed. Separate facilities
not equal." If the case is decided on some trivial basis in
favor of the complaining parties, they go home content but
the sponsoring organization is back where it was in the beginning, shopping for a vehicle to carry a large issue of public policy to the high court.

Some of the frustrations are illustrated in a case in which
the ACLU had participated in Oklahoma several months
earlier as a friend of the court. Jesse M——, white, and
Frances J——, Negro, had been denied a marriage license
under an antimiscegenation statute similar to Virginia's. The
Oklahoma Supreme Court avoided the constitutional challenge sought by the ACLU by disposing of the case on
minor grounds, saying implausibly that a constitutional ruling would be inappropriate before the United States Supreme Court had taken definitive action. The court contended that whatever the merits of the argument about
race, the defendants could not have a license because they
had not complied with all of the state's health and age requirements. Because M—— was only nineteen, said the
court, state law required that his parents consent to his marriage, and they had not. Furthermore, M—— had not taken
the standard premarital physical examination. By Oklahoma
law the consent and examination requirements may be
waived if the female is pregnant or has given birth to an illegitimate child *and* if the parties are twenty-five or older.
Miss J—— was indeed pregnant at the time, and in fact had
lived with M—— for some time and was the mother of two
children by him—but neither of the two was twenty-five.

Therefore no marriage.[38] Within days, as the case was prepared for appeal to the United States Supreme Court, M——married a white girl and the ACLU's test case evaporated. Federal courts will not accept hypothetical cases.

Perhaps the best known sponsor of civil rights test cases is the NAACP, along with its Legal Defense and Educational Fund, but in the *Loving* case they took a supporting role, in the last stage. A clue to the relatively modest interest of black organizations in the miscegenation issue may be Gunnar Myrdal's "rank order of discrimination" as set forth in *An American Dilemma,* first published in 1944. The Swedish savant reviewed American race relations meticulously, and concluded that what was most important to the discriminatory white man was least important among possible discriminations to the black man, and vice versa. From the point of view of the white man, said Myrdal, intermarriage and sexual relations between black men and white women were of the highest concern, followed in importance by social intercourse, segregation of schools and other facilities, political disfranchisement, discrimination in courts and by police, and finally discrimination in employment and welfare. To the black man, he said, job and business opportunity headed the list, with intermarriage at the very bottom.[39] If this is so, what is most likely to arouse white racist ire—any move to put an end to laws against mixed marriage—is least likely to be championed by Negro civil rights organizations. Also, if this is so, it is probably not accidental that the Lovings' case was fought through the appellate courts not by the NAACP but by the American Civil Liberties Union, a largely white organization of liberals, whose emphasis has been on securing freedom of expression and association and procedural, court-related rights, not on matters of race. In a 1963 television interview, Roy Wilkins of the NAACP had explained the lack of enthusiasm in his organization for a frontal attack on state antimiscegenation laws:

. . . We've moved into that area some time ago. We have secured, for example, the repeal of a number of laws that formerly existed in some of the other states. This is a continuing program of ours on which we do not place high priority and, therefore, it isn't pursued with intensity, but it is pursued.

He gave higher priority to voting, equal justice, equal education, and "above all" equal access to jobs.[40] (The NAACP and its Legal Defense and Educational Fund did submit briefs in the *Loving* case as friends of the court, as we shall see, and provided counsel for appellants in the case that killed Florida's interracial cohabitation statute.) Of course the antimiscegenation laws, despite their narrow impact and their low practical importance to Negroes, had a good deal of symbolic meaning for both races.

A paradox of judicial review in the United States is that the Supreme Court normally refuses to take cases that in its opinion do not involve real interests and actual disputes and also will not take cases for their own peculiar merits, but rather for their wider implications instead. And so it was legally vital that the Lovings were suffering materially from the application of Virginia's laws and also that many others were in the same predicament, in Virginia and other states.

Each of the organizations submitting briefs to the Supreme Court had to show that its members had a direct interest in the outcome of the case in order to qualify as a friend of the court. In recent years, swamped by briefs, the Supreme Court has turned away those with only a philosophical concern, who did not have the written consent of the litigants.[41] The NAACP would have no difficulty on either score, but it went through the formality of describing its membership and structure (a New York membership corporation with approximately fifteen hundred local affiliates in fifty states and the District of Columbia, etc.) before presenting its arguments. The information in the NAACP brief was interesting and likely to be useful to the Court in reaching and substantiating a decision against the antimiscegenation laws. It included data about past and present coverage of the laws (Indiana and Wyoming had repealed theirs as recently as 1965) and suggested a distinction between marriage laws based on race and those based on feeblemindedness or disease: unlike the miscegenation laws, the latter are "supported by demonstrable knowledge that such marriages present a potential danger to society through physically or mentally ill offspring."

The NAACP Legal Defense and Educational Fund described itself as a New York nonprofit membership corporation formed to assist Negroes to secure their constitutional rights by prosecution of lawsuits. In the course of its argument the fund struck blows at the straw men mentioned above—the old cases from Missouri, Alabama, and other states "proving" that miscegenation results in sterile or effeminate progeny.

The Japanese American Citizens League emphasized that their organization was open to all, irrespective of race and national origin, and consisted mainly of some twenty thousand persons of Japanese ancestry across the nation. To show the interest of its members and Japanese-Americans in general, it pointed out that of the 464,332 Japanese-Americans counted in the 1960 census, 17,911 were in states with antimiscegenation laws, including 1,733 in Virginia. Many of the 17,911 would be affected by state laws forbidding white-Oriental marriage. Only Georgia, the brief stated, mentioned Japanese specifically, but a number referred to Orientals or Mongolians. This brief too hit at some of the more conservative state decisions of the last century, such as this one from Georgia:

> Equality does not exist and never can. The God of ·
> nature made it otherwise and no human law can pro-
> duce it and no human tribunal can enforce it.

In presenting the Missouri sterile-progeny quotation, the
JACL brief contended that it was not brought up for shock
value: "The quotation is significant not because it now appears so ludicrous but because it suggests that only 80 years
ago it was thought that Negroes and whites were different
species incapable of intermingling to create fertile progeny."
If this were indeed so, there would have been little anxiety
about miscegenation and no antimiscegenation laws.

Finally among the friends of the court on the Lovings'
side were the National Conference for Interracial Justice,
the National Catholic Social Action Conference, and sixteen
bishops of the Roman Catholic church. The Catholic brief
cited Catholic and other denominations' views that marriage is a religious sacrament deserving special protection
from state interferences. It brought up a 1943 flag-salute
case in which the Supreme Court had said that the First
Amendment freedoms, including free exercise of religion,
are "susceptible of restriction only to prevent grave and im-
mediate danger to interests which the state may lawfully
protect." And in keeping with the current trend toward dis-
covery of new family rights in the roomy interstices of the
Bill of Rights and the Fourteenth Amendment, the brief
argued that the Virginia laws were unconstitutional because
they denied the right to beget children.

Catholic opinion had not always been brought to bear on
this side of the issue in the Supreme Court. A few years earlier, Father John LaFarge's *The Race Question and the
Negro* had been cited at length in a miscegenation case in
favor of antimiscegenation law. Father LaFarge's point had
been not that a legal prohibition was required, but that in
most instances racial intermarriage was immoral because of

the difficulty of establishing normal social relationships in such circumstances. If marriage could be undertaken by people of different races in total isolation from others no moral difficulty would arise, but normally marriage partners "bring with them into the orbit of married life their parents and brothers and sisters and uncles and aunts and the entire social circle in which they revolve. All of these are affected by the social tension, which in turn reacts upon the peace and unity of the marriage bond" and has its harshest effect on the children.

On the other side, the brief of North Carolina as a friend of the court added nothing of consequence to Virginia's case.

The Supreme Court was now ready to listen to oral arguments before retiring to consider the Lovings' case in the light of more than a century of constitutional tradition.

5

The Constitution Undergoes a Change

Constitutional protection for men and women subjected to state and local race laws had increased greatly from the beginning of the republic to 1967, when the *Loving* case was argued. Before the Civil War the United States Constitution condoned slavery and all lesser forms of racial discrimination. In the *Dred Scott* case in 1857, notably, Chief Justice Roger Taney cited state miscegenation laws as evidence that Negroes were low in status and unfit for citizenship and the other privileges of whites:

> They show that a perpetual and impassable barrier was intended to be erected between the white race and the one which they had reduced to slavery, and governed with absolute and despotic power, and which they looked upon as so far below them in the scale of created beings, that intermarriages between white persons and negroes or mulattoes were regarded as unnatural and immoral, and punished as crimes, not only in the parties, but in the person who joined them in marriage. And no distinction in this respect was made between the free negro and mulatto and the slave, but this stigma, of the deepest degradation, was fixed upon the whole race.[1]

Only Maine among the states of the union was found by Taney to have made no declaration of black inferiority of any kind.

The Civil War Amendments

The Civil War Amendments freed the slaves and gave all people, regardless of race, a measure of legal equality:

> Amendment XIII: Neither slavery nor involuntary servitude, except as a punishment for crime whereof of the party shall have been convicted, shall exist within the United States, or any place subject to their jurisdiction. . . .
>
> Amendment XIV: All persons born or naturalized in the United States, and subject to the jurisdiction thereof, are citizens of the United States and of the State wherein they reside. No State shall make or enforce any law which shall abridge the privileges or immunities of citizens of the United States; nor shall any State deprive any person of life, liberty, or property, without due process of law; nor deny to any person within its jurisdiction the equal protection of the laws. . . .
>
> Amendment XV: The right of citizens of the United States to vote shall not be denied or abridged by the United States or by any State on account of race, color, or previous condition of servitude.

The most obvious guarantees of general legal equality among these words are the Thirteenth—antislavery— Amendment itself and the equal protection and privileges and immunities clauses of the Fourteenth Amendment. But the Supreme Court in its role as final arbiter of the meaning of the Constitution has at times reduced these rights to

empty phrases for the Negro and then on occasion made use
of other words in the Civil War Amendments to combat racial discrimination. There has been no overall logic or consistency in interpretation during the century of the life of
these amendments, and the history of the enactment of the
amendments is sufficiently clouded with ambiguity and
contradiction to allow partisans of both broad and narrow
interpretation to claim historical legitimacy for their present
preferences.

The strongest interpretive disagreement has occurred on
the question of whether the Civil War Amendments were
meant to define and protect property rights or nonproperty
rights primarily—in other words, whether they were intended to benefit businessmen or Negroes first. By constru-
ing the Thirteenth and Fifteenth Amendments narrowly
(and the privileges and immunities clause of the Fourteenth
similarly) and turning the due process and equal protection
clauses into a businessmen's defense against state welfare
and regulatory legislation, the judiciary for a time nearly
eliminated the racial content of the three amendments. The
antislavery amendment was held to be little more than a
declaration of the abolition of slavery and not to encompass
any kind of discrimination short of slavery. (Later generations were to find that military conscription was not included either, although the words fit.) The voting amendment was rendered useless for a time by narrow construction—blacks might bring cases of voting discrimination
to court and satisfy a hostile judge that the complainants
were black and that they had been denied the right to vote,
only to run up against the judge's fatal demand that they
prove the discrimination occurred *because* they were black.

The Fourteenth Amendment was gutted. The Supreme
Court gave the privileges and immunities clause the permanent status of a truism in the *Slaughterhouse Cases* by distin-
guishing between the rights of state and national citizenship

and bringing only a small list of the latter under the protection of the amendment.[2] The remaining clauses of the Fourteenth Amendment, apart from the definition of citizenship, were turned to the defense of property. Of the three values in the due process clause—life, liberty, and property —life was found largely irrelevant, liberty became liberty of contract, and property was interpreted to include the profits a business firm could make if it were not subjected to rate-fixing and other regulations. Corporations were found by the courts to be "persons," in effect, and the beneficiaries, along with other businesses, of this construction. The equal protection clause was also widely employed by the courts to strike down regulatory legislation for containing unreasonable classifications, and since the reasonableness of the scope and nature of a regulation was always a matter of opinion, judges acquired vast discretion to void state legislation and administrative orders.

The deep contempt the conservative judiciary felt for personal rights in the new constitutional provisions was displayed in a miscegenation case in Indiana in 1871. Brushing aside a mixed couple's contention that the Indiana criminal statute violated the Fourteenth Amendment and an enabling federal civil rights act guaranteeing freedom of contract without regard to race (a point that may have been argued in an attempt to speak the judge's language) the court said:

> The fourteenth amendment contains no new grant of power from the people, who are the inherent possessors of all power, to the Federal government. It did not enlarge the powers of the Federal government, nor diminish those of the States. The inhibitions against the States doing certain things have no force or effect. They do not prohibit the States from doing any act that they could have done without them.

> The people of this State have declared that they are
> opposed to the intermixture of races, and all amalga-
> mation. If the people of other States desire to permit
> corruption of blood, and a mixture of races, they have
> the power to adopt such policy.[3]

Gradually the Supreme Court abandoned these pro-prop-
erty attitudes in favor of others that aided minorities and
criminal defendants. In the 1930s and 1940s businesses lost
their constitutional immunities from regulation. Meanwhile
the Court was softening its predecessors' views of racial discrimination. In education and other public services the separate-but-equal doctrine of *Plessy* v. *Ferguson*,[4] which legalized segregated facilities, gradually gave way to the
doctrine of *Brown* v. *Board of Education* [5] that segregated
facilities are inherently unequal. The equal protection
clause of the Fourteenth Amendment and the Fifteenth
Amendment as a whole became strong weapons for the advancement of civil rights. They grew to be more nearly
what civil rights proponents of the last century insisted the
amendments were originally meant to be.

Another great interpretive dispute has affected antimiscegenation laws only indirectly: the question of whether private racial discrimination was meant to be outlawed by the
Civil War Amendments, and the related question whether
the Thirteenth or the Fourteenth Amendment should carry
the main burden of prohibiting discrimination. In 1883, the
same year it upheld an Alabama law attaching heavy penalties for conviction of interracial fornication, the Supreme
Court struck down sections of a federal civil rights statute
which outlawed discrimination in inns, theaters, and other
places of public accommodation. The Court held that the
Fourteenth Amendment was intended to reach public but
not private discrimination.[6] Upholding the Alabama law

and striking down the federal law were actions consistently unsympathetic to the claims of blacks.

At the time of the *Loving* decision, the judiciary was moving toward repudiation of the public-private distinction of 1883. One of its strategies, in addition to changing the meaning of the Fourteenth Amendment, was the revival of the Thirteenth as a broad guarantee of equality above and beyond the abolition of slavery. An explanation of the Court's reliance on the Thirteenth rather than the Fourteenth Amendment in 1968 as a basis for open housing may be that the long history of scrupulously restrictive interpretation of the Fourteenth Amendment made revival of the Thirteenth simpler, since there was very little case law built on it. Had the history of interpretation of the Civil War Amendments been different, or if the Lovings had raised their complaint before the Supreme Court some years later, the antislavery amendment rather than the equal protection and due process clauses might have been the basis of decision.

Antimiscegenation laws are tested

Once the movement toward legal provision of certain equal rights for Negroes had gotten under way, as signalled by *Brown* v. *Board of Education,* it is a curiosity that it took so long—from 1954 to 1967—to strike down state laws discriminating in a matter so fundamental as the choice of marital partner. Compliance with *Brown* in the public schools has been painfully slow, though, and so perhaps one should not have expected an easy extension of the spirit of the decision to other kinds of racial discrimination. Five years after *Brown,* one surly court in Louisiana in *sustaining* an antimiscegenation law even taunted the Supreme Court with a quotation from Chief Justice Warren's opinion. Louisiana's statute, said the court, helped to maintain racial purity and prevent the propagation of half-breed children who would be unsuited to fit into society. "Children in such a situation are burdened, as has been said in another connection, with 'a feeling of inferiority as to their status in the community that may affect their hearts and minds in a way unlikely ever to be undone.' " [7]

Perez v. Lippold

Until 1948, no state or federal court had found an antimiscegenation law unconstitutional on any ground. In that year, in the case of *Perez* v. *Lippold*, the Supreme Court of California struck down a provision of the state's civil code which read, "All marriages of white persons with Negroes, Mongolians, members of the Malay race or mulattoes are illegal and void . . . ," as a violation of the guarantee of equal protection of the laws.[8] The petitioners, Andrea Perez, white, and Sylvester D——, black, had argued that as Roman Catholics they had a right to marry under the constitutional guarantee of the free exercise of religion and that the county clerk, Lippold, should not have denied them a marriage license. The court accepted their conclusion but supplied its own logic.

The California statute dated from 1872. In its original form it referred only to the marriage of whites with Negroes or mulattoes, but it had been adjusted in later years to conform to popular views in the state about the undesirability of Orientals. Clerk Lippold's attorneys argued in court that there was no discrimination because all *groups* were equally affected, that is, that whites as well as blacks were subject to the law's prohibitions. The court countered that *individuals* have a right to equal treatment under the law, and that if a *white* man can marry a white woman, a *black* man should be able to also.

Lippold cited an old Missouri case, in which the judge had made an appalling pronouncement: "It is stated as a well authenticated fact that if the issue of a black man and a white woman, and a white man and a black woman intermarry, they cannot possibly have any progeny, and such a fact sufficiently justifies those laws which forbid the intermarriage of blacks and whites, laying out of view other sufficient grounds for such enactments." The court felt that modern opinion disagreed with this "fact," as well as with an 1869 Georgia opinion Lippold quoted: "The amalgamation of the races is not only unnatural, but is always productive of deplorable results. Our daily observation shows us that the offspring of these unnatural connections are . . . inferior in physical development and strength to the full blood of either race." The California court said it would make no difference as a matter of law if the Missouri and Georgia theories *were* correct. To Lippold's contention that miscegenationists come from the "dregs of society" and that their progeny would be a burden on the community, the court replied that no law may forbid marriage among the dregs of society.[9]

Clearly the biological arguments in favor of antimiscegenation laws are the kind few educated people take seriously today, yet one dissenting judge in the *Perez* case echoed the old myths presented by Lippold's counsel: ". . . there is authority for the conclusion that the crossing of the primary races leads gradually to retrogression and to eventual destruction of the resultant type unless it is fortified by reunion with the parent stock. . . . Gregory states that where two such races are in contact the inferior qualities are not bred out, but may be emphasized in the progeny, a principle widely expressed in modern eugenic literature." A more credible view was expressed in an opinion by a member concurring with the majority, who quoted at length from Adolf Hitler's writings ("All that is not race in this world is trash," and so forth) and concluded that foreign and domestic racism were disreputable intellectually and morally.[10]

The Lovings' counsel knew their case was strongest on humanitarian grounds and weakest in that a decision against the Virginia antimiscegenation conviction required repudiation of long-standing laws of many states, of court decisions sustaining the laws, and of the Court's own tradition of noninterference with antimiscegenation laws. Although the members differ sharply on the point, the Court as a whole tends to be reluctant to change directions abruptly. Instead, where it seems to have no better choice, it may dodge the issue, as it had done twice lately in the case of miscegenation, or abandon precedent and blandly pretend otherwise (*Dennis* v. *United States* and *Gideon* v. *Wainwright* are notable examples [11]) in order to maintain the appearance of a seamless legal web and a proper respect for the wisdom of the past. If the Supreme Court were to decide for the Lovings, it would have to deal with the precedent of *Jackson* v. *Alabama* (1954), *Naim* v. *Naim* (1956), and *McLaughlin* v. *Florida* (1964).[12]

McLaughlin v. Florida

In *McLaughlin* the Supreme Court struck down a Florida law against sexual relations between whites and blacks, but declined an invitation to rule on the constitutionality of a companion statute forbidding racial intermarriage. The NAACP Legal Defense and Education Fund had gone to the Supreme Court with the case of Dewey McLaughlin, black, a native of British Honduras, and Connie H——, white, a waitress from Alabama, hoping to test the broad issue rather than the single statutory provision. The defendants were discovered together in a Miami Beach apartment in 1961 after Miss H——'s landlady, Dora G——, began to suspect that a black man was living on the premises, confirmed her suspicion forthwith by viewing McLaughlin unclothed in the bathroom, and called the police.[13] She testified in the ensuing trial that Connie H—— had registered for the apartment with a white man but in fact had been living with McLaughlin. The couple were sentenced to 30 days in jail and fined $150 each under a provision of the law establishing a presumption that habitual occupancy of the same room by persons of the opposite sex is tantamount to sexual relations. They had served most of the sentence before their release on bond pending appeal.[14]

The Florida high court, in a caustic opinion by Justice Millard Caldwell, dared the Supreme Court to overrule both it and *Pace* v. *Alabama* (1883), which upheld a statute punishing interracial adultery and fornication more heavily than intraracial. Said Caldwell:

> This appeal is a mere way station on the route to the United States Supreme Court, where defendants hope that, in the light of supposed social and political advances, they may find legal endorsement of their ambitions. . . . If the newfound concept of "social justice" has outdated "the law of the land," . . . it must be enacted by legislative process or some other court must write it.

In its appearance before the Supreme Court, Florida tried to narrow the issue by contending that the defendants were being punished for immorality, not for race, while the counsel for defendants tried to broaden it by bringing in the racial intermarriage statute, arguing that it prevented the couple from defending their behavior on the ground that they had established a common law marriage:

Appellants were denied rights under the due process
and equal protection clauses of the Fourteenth Amendment by Florida's miscegenation laws which had the
effect of requiring the jury to disregard evidence of a
common law marriage if it decided that one appellant
was white and the other was Negro.

The State of Florida argued in return:

It is well known that both the white and the negro
races tend to shun the offspring of interracial marriages. Such marriages therefore have the ability of
causing such tension as to be conducive to racial conflict; each race resents the invasion. It is further apparent that proper legislative purpose is provided by the
need to protect the offspring of marriages.

When Florida's lawyers contended that Congress had
meant to exclude black-white miscegenation from the coverage of the Fourteenth Amendment, Chief Justice Warren
asked, "Could a state do the same with Jews and Gentiles?"
"No sir." "Why not?" "The Constitution did not have that
intention, and we say the intention was expressed as to Negroes and whites. . . . No matter how abhorrent it is to us,
we should recognize the intention of the framers of the
amendment." [15]

Writing in the *New Republic*, Alexander Bickel of the
Yale Law School had expressed a hope that the Court
would confine itself to the issue of cohabitation and not
raise a storm over "an issue that is, after all, hardly of central importance in the civil rights struggle." [16]

The Supreme Court overruled *Pace* from a middle position, deciding on the basis of race but leaving open the
question of the constitutionality of intermarriage laws such
as Florida's and Virginia's. The *Harvard Law Review* commented, "Since it is likely that the miscegenation issue will

before long be squarely presented to the Court, the majority was probably correct in refusing to go out of its way to rule on the question in *McLaughlin*." [17] Similarly a student commentator for the *Maryland Law Review* reasoned that ". . . when the issue does appear directly before the court in a justiciable controversy, the validity of such patently unconstitutional statutes will be at an end." [18] Even the *Mississippi Law Journal* concurred, in a student note: ". . . no one can gainsay the probability that the life expectancy of these statutes will be short." [19]

Naim v. Naim

A decade before, only six months after *Brown* v. *Board of Education*, in the case of *Jackson* v. *Alabama*, the Supreme Court had refused to consider a conviction under a racial intermarriage statute,[20] and then a little while later had twice declined to rule on Virginia's antimiscegenation statute. Ham Say Naim, a Chinese seaman, and Ruby Elaine Naim, a Caucasian, had left Virginia on June 26, 1952, to be married in Elizabeth City, North Carolina, and had returned that day to Virginia to live as husband and wife very much as the Lovings were to do several years later. On September 30, 1953, Ruby Naim filed a bill for annulment in Portsmouth, Virginia, where she then resided. Ham Say Naim moved for dismissal on grounds that the marriage was valid in North Carolina and that invalidation in Virginia would violate the Fourteenth Amendment. After a hearing in Portsmouth the marriage was annulled—that is, officially declared not to have existed—and Ham Say Naim appealed to the Supreme Court of Appeals of Virginia. The high court allowed the appeal, invited a brief by the commonwealth attorney general as a friend of the court (in order to have the same interests represented as if the case were criminal, with the individual confronting the state), and upheld the annulment on June 13, 1955, with references to "racial pride" *versus* "a mongrel breed."

David Carliner, who was later to assist the American Civil Liberties Union in handling the final appeal in the *Loving* case, appealed Naim's case to the Supreme Court. On his side were representatives of a number of interest groups: the American Jewish Congress, the Association of American Indian Affairs, the Association of Immigration and Nationality Lawyers, and the Japanese American Citizens League. The Supreme Court, exercising its lawful discretion, refused to make a decision on two occasions, a matter of apparent embarrassment to the Court later on—in the *Loving* opinion, Chief Justice Warren, in the course of citing a great many cases, made no reference at all to the abortive appeals to the Supreme Court by Naim. In this chronology there is a good deal of support for the view that the Supreme Court makes choices between logic and prudence, sometimes favoring one, sometimes the other.

Loving v. *Virginia*

In *Loving*, Virginia Attorney General Button, as at the time of arguing the jurisdictional issue, made a number of points in favor of the state law, all of which were more sophisticated than the poetic flourishes of Judge Bazile or even the Confederate rhetoric which the Supreme Court of Appeals of Virginia turned out for home consumption. First he applied a distinction long a favorite of the more procedure-minded members of the Supreme Court, between the wisdom and the constitutionality of a piece of legislation. With this distinction, a Justice Stone or Frankfurter or Harlan could sustain a questionable statute by affirming the right of the people's representatives to make mistakes, within the broad limits of their powers. Said Button, "Any judicial inquiry into the wisdom, propriety or desirability of preventing interracial alliances is utterly forbidden." Next he contended that the legislative history of the Civil Rights Act of 1866, from which he presented excerpts to show the intended exemption of state antimiscegenation statutes from federal interference, was in effect a guide to the meaning of the Fourteenth Amendment because the Fourteenth adopted some of the language of the act and was meant to affirm the authority of Congress to enact such laws.

Most effectively, Button cited nonsouthern scientific authority for his cause. Gordon's work on intermarriage was read again. "The chances for the success of an interracial marriage are, according to my research, even less than that of an interfaith marriage." And so on. From *Science*, a technical journal of the highest standing, Button quoted 1964 articles by Dwight J. Ingle, Professor of Physiology at the University of Chicago, to the effect that there is no justification for the belief that the races are genetically equal, in the absence of firm supporting evidence. Ingle expressed doubts about encouraging interracial marriage and criticized liberal dogmatists whose views on race, in his opinion, are as unscientific as any of the white supremacists'. And from the February 3, 1967 issue of *Time* magazine, Button presented the story of William S. Shockley's attack on "inverted liberalism," the current taboo on research on genetic differences among races. According to Shockley, a professor at Stanford and a Nobel laureate for his work in the development of the transistor, much remained to be done in sifting out the hereditary and environmental causes of racial differences. For his efforts, said *Time*, Shockley was reviled by his colleagues for seeking "pseudo-scientific justification for class and race prejudice." The story concluded with a comment of David Krech, University of California psychologist, who attributed the dearth of information on the nature of racial differences to problems of scientific measurement rather than taboo.

Button succeeded in showing that some of the scientific questions concerning race were unresolved.

The ACLU assault on Virginia's statutes was similarly comprehensive. On the matter of original meaning, the answer to Button was that the provisions of the Fourteenth Amendment were "open-ended and meant to be expounded in light of changing times and circumstances to prohibit racial discrimination"—a point notables on the Court, including John Marshall and Oliver Wendell Holmes, Jr., had made in their day and one that Chief Justice Warren had reiterated in *Brown* v. *Board of Education* in 1954, to insist that the aspirations of the twentieth century would not be confined by the prejudices of the nineteenth. The lawyers cited Alexander Bickel on the uses of history: ". . . the relevant point is that the Radical leadership succeeded in obtaining a provision whose effect was left to future determination."

ACLU counsel drew a parallel between Virginia's policy, which it characterized as designed in the first place to preserve slavery and kept alive by intolerance, and Adolf Hitler's dream of creating a super race. Antimiscegenation laws, they said, were "legalized racial prejudice, unsupported by reason or morals." The kind of support exemplified by trial judge Leon Bazile in his peroration on Almighty God's plan for the races to stay put, each on its own continent, "requires no comment."

On the scientific front, the ACLU cited a letter to the editor of the *New York Times* of December 15, 1964, from members of the department of Anthropology at Columbia University stating that there is no indication that racial mixing has biologically deleterious results—to the contrary, there is some evidence, particularly in the population of Hawaii, of hybrid vigor in humans paralleling that in other forms of life. The lawyers also pointed to an article by Morton Fried in the *Saturday Review* arguing that scientifically speaking there is no white race.

Then counsel quoted at length from Myrdal's *An American Dilemma* to get to the pith of Virginia's racial policy, legalisms and questions of how equal or unequal aside. In Myrdal's view, the white southern racist's dread of intermarriage is used to rationalize many types of discrimination that have no relation to intermarriage: ". . . what white people really want is to keep the Negroes in a lower status." Their preoccupation with interracial sex and marriage is a way of justifying social discrimination; it is an escape by whites from the making of demands for social status for itself. Furthermore, said Myrdal, "the fixation on the purity of white womanhood, and also part of the intensity of emotion surrounding the whole sphere of segregation and discrimination are to be understood as the backwashes of the sore conscience on the part of white men for their own or their compeers' relations with, or desires for, Negro women."

The Lovings' counsel summed up: "Paradoxical as it may seem that this most blatant ascription of inferior status is the last to be condemned by this Court, it is fitting that the opportunity to make the condemnation universal presents itself."

The next move was the Court's.

On June 12, 1967, in the purple-draped courtroom of the Supreme Court building, which has been variously described as a temple and a mausoleum—but imposing in any case—Chief Justice Warren solemnly announced the decision of a unanimous court. Seven justices joined the chief justice in his "opinion of the court," and one, Potter Stewart, gave separate reasons for finding the Virginia law unconstitutional. As usual, the Court drew heavily on arguments of counsel, but here added matter of its own by selecting some broad libertarian and egalitarian statements from its own

World War II opinions on the relocation of the Japanese-
Americans on the West Coast, making the best of a bad situation, perhaps, but also leading a casual reader to suppose
that the Court had in fact done something then for the be-
leaguered citizens and aliens of Japanese extraction. Said
the Chief Justice:

> This case presents a constitutional question never
> addressed by this Court: whether a statutory scheme
> adopted by the State of Virginia to prevent marriages
> between persons solely on the basis of racial classifica-
> tions violates the Equal Protection and Due Process
> Clauses of the Fourteenth Amendment. For reasons
> which seem to us to reflect the central meaning of
> those constitutional commands, we conclude that these
> statutes cannot stand consistently with the Fourteenth
> Amendment. . . .
> While the state court is no doubt correct in asserting
> that marriage is a social relation subject to the State's
> police power, . . . the State does not contend in its ar-
> gument before this Court that its powers to regulate
> marriage are unlimited notwithstanding the commands
> of the Fourteenth Amendment. . . . Instead, the State
> argues that the meaning of the Equal Protection
> Clause, as illuminated by the statements of the Fram-
> ers, is only that state penal laws containing an inter-
> racial element as part of the definition of the offense
> must apply equally to whites and Negroes in the sense
> that members of each race are punished to the same
> degree. Thus, the State contends that, because its mis-
> cegenation statutes punish equally both the white and
> the Negro participants in an interracial marriage, these
> statutes, despite their reliance on racial classifications,
> do not constitute an invidious discrimination based
> upon race. The second argument advanced by the

State assumes the validity of its equal application theory. The argument is that, if the Equal Protection Clause does not outlaw miscegenation statutes because of their reliance on racial classifications, the question of constitutionality would thus become whether there was any rational basis for a State to treat interracial marriages differently from other marriages. On this question, the State argues, the scientific evidence is substantially in doubt and, consequently, this Court should defer to the wisdom of the state legislature in adopting its policy of discouraging interracial marriages.

Because we reject the notion that the mere "equal application" of a statute containing racial classifications is enough to remove the classifications from the Fourteenth Amendment's proscription of all invidious racial discriminations, we do not accept the State's contention that these statutes should be upheld if there is any possible basis for concluding that they serve a rational purpose. . . .

The State argues that statements in the Thirty-ninth Congress about the time of the passage of the Fourteenth Amendment indicate that the Framers did not intend the Amendment to make unconstitutional state miscegenation laws. . . . We have rejected the proposition. . . .

There can be no question but that Virginia's miscegenation statutes rest solely upon distinctions drawn according to race. The statutes proscribe generally accepted conduct if engaged in by members of different races. Over the years, this Court has consistently repudiated "distinctions between citizens solely because of their ancestry" as being "odious to a free people whose institutions are founded upon the doctrine of equality." . . .

The fact that Virginia only prohibits interracial marriages involving white persons demonstrates that the
racial classifications must stand on their own justification, as measures designed to maintain White Supremacy. . . .

These statutes also deprive the Lovings of liberty
without due process of law in violation of the Due Process Clause of the Fourteenth Amendment. The freedom to marry has long been recognized as one of the
vital personal rights essential to the orderly pursuit of
happiness by free men. . . .

These convictions must be reversed.

It is so ordered.

With the final destruction of Jim Crow legislation, the Supreme Court had in no way completed its work against racial discrimination, of course. Already the Court and its critics in civil rights organizations, law schools, and the press
were turning their attention to more complex and subtle
patterns of discrimination. At the same time the significance
of the *Loving* case diminished under the impact of the separatist ideologies of black militants, who spurned white liberal concessions and viewed integration—of which intermarriage was a prime symbol—as an affront to the black
culture. In the quick dialectic of American race relations,
the *Loving* victory was welcomed with indifference from all
sides. The editorial columns of the *New York Times* took up
some obscure problems of the Upper Selway region in north
central Idaho the next morning, but made no mention of
miscegenation for over a week.

The Impact of Loving

Official reaction

That official reaction to the *Loving* decision was mixed, ranging from acceptance to hostility, is no surprise to those who follow the work of the legal system. Some officers of government, though sworn to uphold the Constitution of the United States, rejected the Court's new view of the law of the land and continued to enforce antimiscegenation statutes; others obeyed the decision as authoritative in Virginia and the remaining states equally; while a few even set about enlarging the meaning of *Loving* in new and unplanned directions. It has always been hazardous to predict the amount and kind of compliance a major constitutional statement will enjoy.[1]

Perhaps with the litigation over school desegregation in mind as a model of the frustration and delay in civil rights that could result from stout resistance on the part of offending areas under an indefinite court decree, even southern legal commentators predicted straightforward acceptance of the Court's clear mandate on intermarriage. Witness these student notes in southern law reviews, differing in tone but together in regarding the *Loving* decision as authoritative:

> Miscegenation laws were a significant stigma of race inferiority; their validity is now at an end. As a

consequence of the instant decision, prosecution for interracial marriages may no longer be instituted. Furthermore, children of such unions will no longer bear the stigma of illegitimacy; they will be able to inherit, and to assume their rightful place in society.[2]

. . . Whatever scheme is created and however nicely it is drawn, it will probably be futile to attempt to enforce it. The *Loving* case represents a basic change in scientific information and social philosophy which will probably persist for many years.[3]

But experience might have indicated the prudence of hedging one's bets. When California's law was struck down by its highest court two decades before *Loving*, a number of registrars refused to drop the question of race from marriage license applications. In one case reported, a Caucasian couple wrote "human" in the space provided, and had to threaten suit to overcome the registrar's objections.[4] After *Loving* there were clerks and registrars who would not issue a license to a mixed couple without a court order, in a manner reminiscent of a southern school board's contention that a desegregation order in Tuscaloosa County had no bearing on the people in Tallapoosa County. Federal courts were called upon to direct compliance in Delaware two weeks after the Supreme Court's decision and in Little Rock, Arkansas, the next year.[5] In Florida the state Supreme Court was obliged to grant a writ of mandamus early in 1968, ordering the issuance of a marriage license to a black man and a white woman after the county court in Miami balked. Curiously, two of the seven judges voting in this case dissented, without giving any reasons, although the strength of feeling of one of the two, Chief Justice Caldwell, was open to public view in the *McLaughlin* opinion as we have seen.[6]

Other states accepted the ruling without a display of opposition. In Oklahoma the state Supreme Court found its antimiscegenation statute unconstitutional within hours of a ruling to that effect by the Oklahoma Attorney General, even though less than a year before the court had declined to act on the question, preferring to let the United States Supreme Court be the first to decide.[7] In Virginia the first modern interracial marriage of record occurred without incident less than two months after *Loving*, when a black gasoline station manager married a white woman in a Jehovah's Witness ceremony in Norfolk.[8]

Perhaps the most memorable of the new mixed marriages took place in Nashville, Tennessee, in July 1967, between a black dishwasher and a white woman five years his senior, both employees of a local motel. The couple accompanied their attorney to the courthouse to apply for a license under the shadow of what proved to be a false rumor that the White Citizens Council would obstruct their efforts. License in hand, with hopes of finding a judge somewhere in the building to perform the ceremony, they attracted a small crowd, which by good fortune included a black Baptist minister kind enough to offer his services. He had no Bible with him, however, and so the wedding was delayed while another bystander went to find one, and returned with a dog-eared copy. They were married promptly while a television crew moved in to record the dialogue and the embrace, and a flustered clerk scurried up calling for a six dollar fee he had neglected to collect in the excitement of making state history minutes before.[9] Two months later, it is sad to relate, the groom was indicted by a Davidson County grand jury for bigamy. The prosecutor produced three marriage licenses and induced the groom to plead guilty when it became clear he could offer no divorce papers in rebuttal.[10] The second mixed marriage in Tennessee was more successful, uniting a white sailor and a Negro girl he had met several months earlier at a naval base dance. The young sailor had served for two years in West Africa with the Peace

Corps before entering the Navy. Both families were present at a quiet wedding ceremony.[11]

After a first few test cases, it was unlikely that applicants for licenses for mixed marriages would encounter much official resistance in northern and border states. In Mississippi compliance with the *Loving* decision was slower. More than three years passed before interracial marriages were attempted openly, and then a legal battle was required to bring the state under the Supreme Court's edict. One mixed couple married quietly in July, 1970.[12] Then a twenty-four-year-old white law clerk from Boston and a young Negro girl from rural southern Mississippi attending Jackson State College applied for a license at the office of Circuit Clerk H. T. Ashford in Jackson, not expecting or encountering any obstruction. During the statutory three-day waiting period, however, a white supremacist organization, the Southern National Party, obtained a temporary injunction from Mississippi Circuit Court Judge Marshall Perry of Granada, preventing the issuance of the license. The young man, a conscientious objector who had come to Mississippi from law school at George Washington University to work for the NAACP Legal Defense and Educational Fund as alternate service approved by his District of Columbia draft board, immediately sought reversal of Judge Perry's ruling in higher state courts, failed, and took the constitutional question into federal district court in Jackson. It was his bad luck to come before Judge Harold Cox, a Kennedy appointee who had gained some attention in legal circles by referring to Negroes in his courtroom as "chimpanzees" and otherwise showing limited sympathy for civil rights claimants. But under pressure from the Fifth Circuit Court of Appeals in New Orleans, Judge Cox handed down an order forcing the issuance of licenses to the complaining couple and to another in the same predicament, a black factory worker and a white girl from Deerfield, Massachusetts, living in Jackson.

The law, he said, "is so perfectly clear that any delay in granting such licenses . . . would be unwarranted and indefensible. . . . The fact that the parties are of different races is no bar. . . ." On August 2, 1970, the ceremony was performed in a black Methodist church before some two hundred guests, largely black, by a white Presbyterian minister, who, like the bride and groom, had been active in civil rights work. He called the marriage "born in the movement." It was "not anything different from what's been happening for years in Mississippi," said the groom. "The only thing that is new is that this is the first time the state of Mississippi has sanctioned it." Mississippi formally repealed its antimiscegenation law in April, 1972.[13]

In November, 1970, in Calhoun County, Alabama, when a white soldier stationed at Fort McClellan and his black fiancée were denied a license by Probate Judge C. Clyde Brittain, the Justice Department went into federal court in Birmingham at the request of the Army, seeking an order for the issuance of the license and a ruling on the constitutionality of the state's constitutional and statutory antimiscegenation provisions.[14] It was the first time the federal government had gone to court in opposition to antimiscegenation laws. Federal attorneys argued that the continuance of the prohibitions in Alabama law put a burden on federal military personnel. Their appearance in court was in the interests of national defense rather than civil rights. Early in December a federal judge found the antimiscegenation sections of Alabama's constitution and statutes in violation of the United States Constitution and ordered state officials to stop enforcing them. The couple, however, in their impatience, crossed the border into Tennessee for a simple wedding without the risk of further litigation and delay. In Alabama, a federal court was obliged to issue a similar order in 1972, nearly five years after *Loving*.[15]

As legal barriers to racial intermarriage fell away in most

of the South, a new legal device that served a related purpose was being tested in a number of communities: sex segregation in the public schools. The separatist implications of
this idea, typically introduced as a component in a school
desegregation plan, as a way of advancing the cause of racial purity by avoiding the development of miscegenous
urges in little children, were denied by public officials who
were taken to federal court on constitutional complaints.
And even though it is known that the benefits of segregation
by sex had not occurred to southern school boards, except
in Macon, Georgia, until federal judges ordered racial integration, the courts thus far have not interfered; but in time
they may demand firm proof that the end of coeducation
has been ordered for educational rather than for racial
ends.[16]

Public opinion polls

The mass social consequences of the *Loving* decision, as
distinguished from official reactions, can be traced in the
thought and action of blacks and whites, both those who
mix and their larger audience. Public opinion polls accumu-
lating over a generation show that small but increasing pro-
portions of the population are willing in an abstract way to
contemplate mixed marriage for themselves and to tolerate
it in others. In the realm of action, figures now suggest that
a limited number of mixed marriages are taking place in
areas where the ban has been lifted and that lynchings and
other forms of direct popular reactions to miscegenation are
diminishing. There are obvious difficulties, however, in re-
lating the *Loving* decision itself in any strict cause-and-ef-
fect manner to changes in societal thinking and behavior. At
most the decision seems to have speeded changes already
underway.

White opinion about miscegenation is softening: a large yet diminishing majority admits its opposition. In 1942 about 92 percent said they would not consider marrying a Negro, a level marginally higher than that in Gallup's more recent related polls. From 1963 to 1966 a slight shift toward permissiveness was noted in Harris Polls in answers to questions about objections to dating by one's teenage child and a Negro and about being upset over the marriage of a close friend or relative to a Negro.[17] Most dramatically, in the closest we come to a before-and-after test of the *Loving* case, a 1970 Gallup Poll reports that approval of criminal antimiscegenation laws fell from 48 to 35 percent nationwide in a five-year period.[18]

Within the white population there are substantial differences in attitude associated with region and with ethnic, religious, and class affiliation. The greatest regional contrasts on all racial matters, of course, are between the South and the rest of the nation. Of southerners, 77 percent have agreed that Negroes have looser morals than whites, for instance, compared with 48 percent of northerners.[19] On the question of state criminal miscegenation laws, 72 percent of southern whites approved in 1965, and in 1970 56 percent in the South approved, compared with 30 percent elsewhere.[20] One survey indicated the greatest permissiveness on questions of interracial dating and marriage in the Pacific states and as expected the least in the South.[21] Among ethnic groups, Italians and other late-arriving Catholic minorities have shown a high degree of prejudice against Negroes.[22] But a 1968 Gallup Poll suggests that Protestants are least tolerant of intermarriage nationally, and that Catholics, Jews, and those with no church affiliation, particularly, are most tolerant.[23] In 1942, on the specific point of whether one would consider marrying a Negro, Jews showed less willingness than either Catholics or Protestants among the whites who were polled.[24]

Class, too, makes a difference: white college students, who tend to be both nonconformist and well above the national average in social and economic status, are far less prejudiced than most others. A *Newsweek* survey a few years ago showed that more than a third of them would have no objection to marrying a Negro and that about half would not mind dating a member of another race, disclosing an easing of attitudes since an earlier survey which reported that 29 percent of college students would consider marrying a Negro and 24 percent would be willing to date or allow a son or daughter to date a Negro.[25] The June 1968 Gallup Poll found antimiscegenationist views associated with a low level of formal education, low income, low-prestige occupations, age, a feeling that life is getting worse rather than better morally, and general disapproval of the Supreme Court.[26] A 1970 Gallup Poll reports that 75 percent of adults with college training disapproved of antimiscegenation laws, while a majority of those with only a grade school education approved the laws.[27]

That the levels of prejudice and distaste for outsiders nurtured in every class and every religious or ethnic group describe a unique pattern in each society is demonstrated by a Gallup Poll conducted in 1968 in cooperation with polling organizations in a dozen other countries. In each country interviewers asked questions about approval or disapproval of marriages between whites and nonwhites, Catholics and Protestants, and Jews and non-Jews. In the United States the percentages approving the marriages were 20, 63, and 59, respectively.[28] The people of the United States were more vehemently opposed to marriages between whites and nonwhites than the respondents in any other country sampled, but were about average with respect to the other two questions. The percentages giving approval in the Netherlands were 51, 48, and 44, by comparison, and in Greece 50, 40, and 32, respectively, very much at odds with the American pattern. The Dutch and Greeks were less concerned about racial than religious mixing.

In the international poll, Swedes had the highest level of tolerance, 67 percent approving marriages of whites and nonwhites, 73 percent approving Catholic-Protestant marriages, and 76 percent those of Jews and non-Jews, a liberality of attitude that may be due in part to the luxury a relatively homogeneous nation enjoys of considering racial and religious friction largely in the abstract.

On all black-white questions, including miscegenation, American public opinion occupies a lonely extreme, with only a few nations such as South Africa for company. World opinion has isolated the deviants, as we can see in the unanimous declaration of the biological equality of the races voted by a convention of anthropologists meeting in Moscow under the auspices of UNESCO. Racial differences, the delegates agreed, were wholly explained by cultural history.

> It has never been asserted that the mixing of the races has played a negative role for mankind as a whole. On the contrary, it has helped to preserve biological ties between groups of people and, consequently, the unity of mankind in its diversity.
>
> Hence there is no biological justification for banning interracial marriages or for any advice aimed at banning them.[29]

But however strong and united it may be, international opinion is not persuasive at home. There is no evidence that disapproval from the outside leads to anything but a stiffening of domestic attitudes. Nor are the views of the Negro minority given much attention by the white majority, even in matters such as equal employment opportunity where black opinion is united. And when black views are as divided and obscure as they are on the subject of miscegenation, their influence is minimal.

Black opinion

Among Negroes there is much equalitarian criticism of any
formal impediment to intermarriage for those who have the
personal inclination to cross color lines: ". . . the impudent
demand that all colored folk shall write themselves down as
brutes by a general assertion of their unfitness to marry
other decent folk," said W. E. B. DuBois, "is a night-
mare." [30] When they find they have reciprocated with
racial exclusions of their own, black equalitarians stop to reconsider as a matter of principle. The story was told a few
years ago of St. Thomas's Episcopal Church in Philadelphia,
perhaps the oldest Negro Episcopal Church in the country,
which voted equal rights to white worshippers. From 1796
until the reform, St. Thomas's had excluded whites from
voting membership, which meant that the white spouse in
each of the church's several mixed families could not participate fully in church affairs. The congregation adopted the
change by unanimous vote.[31]

But even staunch equalitarians may agree with James M.
Nabrit, Jr., former president of Howard University, that intermarriage is a minor civil rights problem which should not
be permitted to divert concern from serious issues.[32] A
study of 721 black families living in Chicago shows a similar
distinction between principle and practice: more than four-
fifths of the black parents would permit their children to
marry whites if they had become attached without parental
knowledge, but one-half of the parents would oppose interracial marriage in general advice to their children and almost none would encourage it.[33]

"I'm not against mixed marriages," said black Mayor
Charles Evers of Fayette, Mississippi, when his white city
attorney married a black man, "but there is a right time and

a right place, and this was not the place." Civil rights leader Evers encouraged the Board of Aldermen to fire the attorney, who soon moved with her husband to Detroit. "I'm not going to let anybody destroy our town," said Evers. "We explained to them we could not afford for such things to go on in our town. We gave them a choice between breaking off their friendship and resigning." There was solid opposition to the interracial romance in the Negro community in Fayette.[34] In 1965, according to a Gallup Poll, 30 percent of the Negroes in the South and 14 percent in the rest of the country were strongly enough opposed to miscegenation to approve the idea of state criminal antimiscegenation laws.[35]

Some blacks are inequalitarian not for reasons of prudence in a threatening environment, however, but as a matter of either prejudice or principle. Pure blacks have been known to look down upon mixed-blood blacks, and those who are interested in building black racial pride may learn to despise their own white ancestry, as Malcolm X did. According to Black Muslim Muhammed Ali, formerly Cassius Clay, "We believe mixed marriages should be prohibited." [36] In fact, contrary to the alarmist views of a few white supremacists, no more than a tenth of the whites in the country believe that Negroes have strong feelings about the right to marry whites, although four-fifths think Negroes feel strongly about the right to vote.[37] There may be more of a meeting of minds than Myrdal described a generation ago. White confidence that blacks will prefer not to marry whites is probably the most important reason for the acceptance of the *Loving* ruling.

The incidence of miscegenation

The most concrete effects of *Loving* will appear in marriage rates in the years to come. Whether the state of the

law can have much effect on the incidence of miscegenation, by discouraging those who might cross racial lines for
marriage or sexual relations with threats of criminal sanc-
tions, as in the past, or encouraging them with an act of repeal or a court decision such as *Perez* or *Loving*, cannot be
told with precision now, though better data may be at hand
shortly.

MISCEGENATION BEFORE THE CIVIL WAR

When slavery was permitted by law, miscegenation was
common despite specific prohibitions. The fact that racial
mixing was practiced by master and slave was hardly a mitigation of the rigors of slavery. In America as in other caste
societies a degree of cultural and biological assimilation re-
sulted not from tolerance but from exploitation of the inferior caste by the superior. Negro women were used for the
pleasure of white men or for what DuBois described as
"polyandry between black women and selected white men on
plantations in order to improve the human stock of strong
and able workers." [38] Concubinage and sexual gratification
are the most obvious explanations of miscegenation under
slavery, but economic exploitation is a matter of record from
the beginning, marginally encouraged or discouraged by
the law of the day. The mulatto children of black women
became slaves themselves and increased the wealth of the
white slaveholders; similarly the offspring of black men who
were slaves and white servants who were not were frequently regarded as slaves too.[39] The promise of committing
the child to slavery was considered a strong deterrent to the
servant.

As slaveholders became procurers for their white servant
girls in order to breed mulatto slaves, however, and trans-
formed the intended legal penalty for the servant into an
economic incentive for the master, the law had to be

amended to free the children in cases in which there was evidence of procuring and to adjust the incentives once more. Antimiscegenation laws enacted to remedy the practice had no apparent effect. As early as 1630, the governor and council in Virginia ordered that a white man by the name of Hugh Davis be whipped "before an assembly of Negroes and others for abusing himself to the dishonor of God and shame of a Christian by defiling his body in lying with a Negro," and commanded that he confess his sins publicly the following Sunday.[40] Fornication with Negroes and intermarriage were declared crimes in Virginia in 1662 and 1691, respectively. Those who disobeyed the law could be fined, forced into servitude for long terms, or banished from the colony.

DuBois estimates that by 1860 a fourth of the blacks in America were of mixed blood and that seventy-five years later, largely by mixing within the black community, fewer than a fourth were without some white ancestry.[41] Today about four-fifths of the Negro population is thought to have some white blood; perhaps one-fifth of those who regard themselves as white have Negro blood.[42]

TRENDS IN INTERRACIAL MARRIAGE

As in times of slavery, miscegenation now occurs lawfully, unlawfully, and in ambiguous relationships in between. Interracial marriage, prostitution, casual intercourse, and rape all contribute to the mixing of the races. Davis and the Gardners in their account of the deep South a generation ago described a latter-day form of concubinage as well, a permanent relation between a white man and a black mistress that matured into a marriage in all but a few key respects: the law forbade a legal marriage, the children remained entirely in the black society of the mother, and the white man kept clear of other social associations with the

black race. But the man in this arrangement assumed many
of the usual obligations of husband and father, and often
lived with his black family at some risk to all.[43]

At the other extreme, there have been well-advertised interracial marriages since slavery involving prominent people
—in states without criminal miscegenation statutes. In more
than a few the Negro partner has been an entertainer. Over
the years, many of the best known Negroes in the United
States have married whites. For example: Frederick Doug-
lass, ex-slave, adviser to presidents, and spokesman for
blacks in the decades following the Civil War, who lost popularity as a black leader when at age 67, in 1884, he married
a white suffragist and writer; Father Divine, religious cult
leader; Walter S. White, long the Executive Secretary of the
NAACP, who looked white and married a white woman;
Congressman Adam Clayton Powell of New York, clergyman and political leader, who married a white woman after
having been married to a Negro; poet LeRoi Jones, who
married a black woman after having been married to a
white; novelist Richard Wright; U. S. Senator Edward W.
Brooke of Massachusetts; James Farmer, once head of
CORE, later an Assistant Secretary of Health, Education,
and Welfare; and entertainers Pearl Bailey, Harry Bela-
fonte, Sammy Davis, Jr., Chubby Checker, Eartha Kitt, Leslie Uggams, and Lena Horne.

In 1967 the daughter of Secretary of State Dean Rusk was
married to a young Negro man in the chapel of Stanford
University. The bride and groom and their families had no
illusions about the difficulties to be faced by an interracial
couple or the political implications of the union. The Episcopal minister who performed the wedding ceremony had
counseled them on the hardships of racial pioneering. The
wedding itself was held away from the Washington, D. C.,
area to avoid the embarrassment of a boycott by officials
with conservative racial views. Louisiana Senator Allen El-

lender's remark would have found support in the capital: "If this had started a hundred years ago, after the Civil War, we would have a mongrel race today."[44] Secretary Rusk, who had risen to the ruling elite from a modest background in Georgia, had a record of quiet, consistent opposition to racism. As a captain in 1941 he worked with Ralph Bunche to integrate an officers' mess in the District of Columbia. He is known to have encouraged liberal racial thinking within his family, and to have lent his support to his daughter's marriage. He notified President Johnson of his willingness to resign if the marriage seemed likely to be a burden to the administration, and discovered that the President would not hear of it.

The marriages on the list of celebrities symbolize emancipation for the black, for the most part, while the Rusk marriage symbolizes emancipation for the white partner. The older pattern represented by the black entertainers, politicians, religious leaders, and other notables who married whites may well be dying out. The lesson they offered, intended or not, was that social emancipation could be gained by "marrying light." The more recent tendency represented by Margaret Rusk Smith suggests that love conquers all, and in the process makes social conventions of racial separation less important to whites than they once were. Racial intermarriage among notables has ceased to be stylish. It has become a matter of personal preference. For the black activist, it is backsliding. Probably the trends in mixed marriage among celebrities are the inverse of those in the population as a whole. The inegalitarian assumption underlying the marriage of black entertainers with whites—that one could demonstrate upward mobility by taking a white spouse— made it an attractive solution for privileged blacks in an era when racial antagonism was highest and racial intermarriage in the society as a whole lowest.

The changing trends in intermarriage since the days of

slavery are difficult to observe because data are scarce and
the number of men and women involved has always been
very small. With the exception of some unusually high rates
reported in Boston between 1900 and 1904, spotty tabulations down to the middle of this century, nearly all from the
northeastern quadrant of the country, indicate that somewhere between every twenty-fifth and every hundredth
marriage involving a Negro was mixed, the probability fluc-
tuating according to time and place.[45] Sociologist Robert
Roberts estimated that fewer than 5 percent of all married
Negroes had non-Negro spouses at the end of this period.[46]
This level of intermarriage expressed as a proportion of all
marriages is low—a fraction of 1 percent—and means in
practice that the typical Negro was likely and the typical
white unlikely to know personally of a mixed marriage. But
the rate of intermarriage at mid-century is a poor indicator
of the real extent of racial mixture in the United States. In
fact, during this era black-white marriage and illicit miscegenation both seem to have been in gradual decline. In the
one locale where figures have been compiled over a long period the trend is clear: in the District of Columbia, interracial marriage declined from the 1920s to the 1940s.[47] A
number of other studies suggest (without proving) that this
has generally been true.[48]

Then at mid-century whites and blacks started to intermarry more frequently. In the 1950s a slight but significant
increase was noted in California and a pronounced increase
in Los Angeles specifically.[49] A rise in intermarriage has
been reported in Hawaii, Michigan, Nebraska, and New York
City,[50] and U. S. Census returns show a comparable increase for the nation as a whole.[51] According to the 1960
census, the latest data available at the time of writing, one-
eighth of one percent of all married couples in the United
States now are Negro-white. The prevalence of interracial
couples is relatively greater in the South (.16 percent), and

in descending order less prevalent in the northeast (.13 percent), the West (.10 percent), and the north-central states (.08 percent). The census data show that a smaller proportion of Negroes in the South than in other regions have married whites, but the ratio of mixed marriages to all marriages is highest in the South, because there are relatively more Negroes there.[52] Common sense inclines us to suspect that nonsouthern Negroes would be more apt than southern to marry whites; the surprising fact in the census report is that over twenty thousand inside the South have done so. The South as defined by the census in 1960 was virtually covered by antimiscegenation laws: only the District of Columbia was exempt.

There is every reason to believe that the census figures underestimate the extent of interracial marriage. Census enumerators have always missed a disproportionate number of Negroes, for one thing, and it seems likely that members of mixed households would be unusually reluctant to identify the race of everyone in the family with accuracy. Most of the earlier figures have been based on marriage licenses, which are also of uncertain value. In the District of Columbia some couples listed as interracial on marriage licenses have proved not to be, and some light-skinned Negroes apparently have taken full advantage of the space on the District of Columbia application for "color" (rather than the less ambiguous "race") by writing "white." [53] In New York City, some applicants have filled in "chartreuse," "aquamarine," "red," "flesh," and so forth.

The extent to which mixed marriages are unrecorded because one of the partners is passing as white (or as black) is unknown. W. E. B. DuBois—who, incidentally, regarded Alexander Hamilton as a passer—said, "There is scarcely an American, certainly none of the South and no Negro American, who does not know in his personal experience of Americans of Negro descent who either do not know or do not

acknowledge their African ancestry." [54] Demographers believe that passing has declined since 1900, but estimate that
more than half a million marriages are miscegenous today,
most of them without the knowledge of those involved, because of generations of passing.[55]

For all these reasons, data concerning the prevalence of
intermarriage should be used with care. The same is true
when existing data are broken down by age, class, and the
other characteristics of the people who have entered into
mixed marriage.

More often than not it has been black men and white
women who have married, rather than white men and black
women, although of course the opposite has been true of
miscegenation outside of marriage. A Philadelphia sample
for the years 1922 to 1947 shows that black male–white female marriages were 58.5 percent of the total,[56] and this sta-
tistic is corroborated by figures from Baltimore for 1950
through 1964.[57] In California, for the last years in which racial data were gathered, 1955 through 1959, Negro grooms
were more than three times as prevalent as white in mixed
marriages.[58] Louis Wirth and Herbert Goldhamer specu-
lated that attractive black males may have gained in self-esteem by marrying whites, but that attractive black women
have been inclined to feel that the greater rewards stem
from marriage into the upper economic reaches of black society.[59] Roberts emphasizes instead that white men have
been discouraged from intermarrying for fear that miscegenation would hurt their chances of success in business.

The reversal of this pattern was disclosed in the 1960 national census: mixed couples with white husbands outnum-
bered those with black husbands by the narrow margin of
25,913 to 25,496. In the South the husband is more likely to
be white, by 11,808 to 8,624; elsewhere he is likely to be
black.[60] Furthermore separate census analysis shows a
strong correlation between urban residence and black hus-

bands in mixed marriages, and between suburban or rural residence and white husbands.[61] One student of racial inter-marriage theorizes that the frequency of white male–black female marriage remains fairly constant while black males and white females marry with less predictable frequency.[62] Whether or not this is so, the differences between the South and the remainder of the country, and related rural-urban differences, are consistent with Merton's hypothesis that caste lines will tend to be broken by upper-caste men in America, where the society's sex morality allows the man to make the advances. Outside the South, where caste lines are less rigid, the singular role of the white male in intermarriage is less pronounced.[63]

But in Virginia during the last half of 1967, after the *Loving* decision, seventeen black-white mixed marriages took place, of which thirteen were between black men and white women. The following year, there were thirty-two mixed marriages, twenty-one involving black men and white women.[64] Thus the typically southern race-sex ratio has not been maintained in Virginia's new legal miscegenous marriages. It is easily imaginable that this northern pattern will spread through the South if and when old inhibitions wear away.

There are class patterns in interracial marriage. As in the case of sex ratios, variations occur from region to region and from one generation to the next, discouraging generalization from anything short of a national sample. A special census study of mixed couples in 1960, limited to those married between 1950 and 1960 and married only once, indicated that Negro wives of white husbands were likely to be more educated than their husbands, but that white wives were educationally about equal, on the average.[65] Some of the meaning of these figures can be traced to differences in education by sex within racial groups, yet if education is taken as an index of class, these findings throw doubt on the standard

assumptions that women "marry up" more than men and
that blacks "marry up" more than whites.[66] The census data
also raise questions about the theory that mixed marriage
occurs most often "in the lower and upper extremes of social
status, where the social penalties are least severe." [67] Merton's view, based on sparse data from the urban northeast,
that the typical pattern of racial intermarriage in the United
States is between lower-class white women and higher-class
Negro men turns out to be inappropriate today in all respects for the wider population.[68]

Other studies suggest that miscegenous marriage partners
are more likely than others to have been married previously
and—a related point—are slightly older than average at the
time of marriage. They are far less likely to be wed in religious ceremonies, perhaps in part because they rather often
have different religious backgrounds.[69] And in the past at
least, some mixed marriages have been between American
Negro servicemen overseas and natives of countries with
low levels of racial prejudice or between Negroes in the
United States and immigrants from places such as northern
Europe who did not share or even comprehend the depth of
American disapproval of miscegenation.[70]

It would be interesting to know how well mixed marriages fare, compared with homogeneous unions. The few
studies that have been made of failure rates come to contradictory conclusions, so we await better evidence. The
stresses of such marriages in some cases strengthen the ties
of husband, wife, and children to one another. It is known
that mixed couples may suffer the rejection of both the
white and the black communities. While it is true that the
children of mixed parents are black, according to American
custom, the parents occupy an indeterminate position. They
may live in areas that are black or mixed—Harlem or
Greenwich Village, for example—or in public housing, but
even there not enter into the society. Some indication of

the social isolation of mixed couples is seen in the phenomena of interracial dances and mixed-marriage clubs in large
cities such as Washington, D. C., Detroit, Los Angeles, and
New York.[71] To some, especially the white partners, the societal response to miscegenation can be a grievous disap-
pointment.

Working in favor of intermarriage is what one student of
the matter calls romantic individualism.[72] Some are drawn
into mixed marriage by the excitement and display of inde-
pendence that is involved in crossing the color line. Some
are adhering to family tradition.[73] But for many the evidence is that the bonds of love and marriage have proved
too strong for adverse social pressure. In a society without
traditions of romantic individualism a consensus in favor of
racial separation would be more potent. In the United
States, if large numbers of whites and blacks meet, some
will surely marry. Integrationists and segregationists alike
know that integration brings intermarriage.

Indirectly, the integration of public and parochial schools
fosters intermarriage by weakening the taboo against social
contact, and integration of adult institutions of work and
recreation, and of neighborhoods, leads to the same end
more directly. The civil rights movement itself has brought
men and women of different races together. In 1964, a
young white Student Non-Violent Coordinating Committee
worker, who had the distinction of being charged with fo-
menting insurrection in Georgia and serving four months in
jail without bond until the insurrection statute was declared
unconstitutional, was married outside the state of Georgia
to a black girl, with the intention of returning to work with
SNCC despite the illegality of mixed marriage in the state
at the time.[74] In 1968 a former legislative assistant to Robert
Kennedy was wed to the first black woman to be admitted
to the Mississippi bar, in a ceremony performed by Yale's
chaplain, the Rev. William Sloane Coffin, Jr., and attended

by Associate Justice Arthur Goldberg, Burke Marshall, Joseph L. Rauh, Jr., and other liberals of note. The couple had
met in the spring of 1967 in Mississippi while he was with
Senator Kennedy conducting hearings on hunger. She had
been congressional liaison for the Southern Christian Leadership Conference and later the chief legal adviser to the
Poor People's Campaign.[75] Their wedding in McLean, Virginia, was the commonwealth's most publicized since the
Lovings'.

THE FUTURE

What of the future? Public opinion is venturing tenta-
tively in the direction of tolerance. But racial segregation
persists in many situations where social contacts might lead
to marriage. Civil rights workers are less integrated now
than in the sixties. Employers have shown great powers of
resistance to equal opportunity programs. School integration
has slowed, and President Nixon's declared policy of ending
de jure school segregation while leaving *de facto* segregation untouched promised to keep black and white students
from moving much closer together. It remains to be seen
how seriously the Supreme Court's April 1971 decision allowing busing to eliminate *de jure* segregation will affect
the course of school desegregation.[76] The Court avoided the
more difficult and controversial question of the status of *de
facto* segregation.

De facto segregation in the schools stems from the presence of neighborhood schools in areas where homes are racially segregated. If whites and blacks live in separate
neighborhoods, their children will have little socialization in
interracial living, and the marriageable adults will have less
opportunity to meet and to consider marriage. A study of
interracial marriage in Washington, D. C., stresses the significance of living close: a substantial part of the people

studied had lived at the same address before their marriage, and many more had lived near one another.[77] Yet nationwide there is no trend at all toward residential integration. To the contrary, segregation has been remarkably stable in recent decades, as the Kerner Commission reported, and in the South whites have fled mixed neighborhoods in order to maintain a lawfully segregated neighborhood school system.[78] Little Rock, Arkansas, for example, has become a residentially segregated city since the dramatic integration of Central High School by federal troops in 1957.[79] Romantic individualism is held in check when men and women of different races are infrequently brought together by the institutions of the society.

During the time of slavery and even afterwards in the special relationships of concubinage, prostitution, and escapist or rebellious marriage, physical and social separation of the races could be said more to encourage than to discourage miscegenation. Sexual relationships with members of a lower racial caste in the poorer parts of town might be perceived as less costly socially and monetarily and considerably more provocative than intraracial relations. Physical and social integration are increasingly responsible for interracial marriages, however, between men and women who attract one another despite race or without regard to race. In the same way, equalization of the status of blacks and whites and intermarriage are certain to be mutually enhancing. The older theory that racial mixing was most likely to be undertaken by people of different social status, notably lower-class white women and higher-class (but lower-caste) black men, now seems to be valid only for the special circumstances of the northeastern metropolis of a generation or two ago.

Among the determinants of intermarriage, the state of the law of marriage is important but not at all decisive. Where it is forbidden, mixed marriage nonetheless occurs. In Cali-

fornia a mild antimiscegenation statute did not prevent
mixed marriage.[80] A study of interracial marriage in Indiana, where there was a severe criminal statute, proved that
even the threat of prosecution could not discourage everyone from open marriage.[81] In addition, in California and
elsewhere, even in Mississippi, common-law marriages of
varying degrees of secretiveness occurred before the law
was voided.[82] After racial marriage became legal by legislative or judicial action there was no dramatic change in marriage statistics.[83]

Law is not everything.

The Implications of Loving

When the sexually permissive production of *Che!* opened in New York, *Loving* had no apparent part to play, but before very long the legality of the performance was questioned in court and an enterprising attorney thought of a way to forge the decision into a weapon against censorship. The producers of *Che!* were prosecuted for violation of the state's consensual sodomy statute, which covers acts of oral and anal sodomy. On appeal to the federal district court, three arguments were attempted: first, that the anatomical displays were a part of an artistic whole protected by the First Amendment, a consideration rejected out of hand by the court; second, that whatever sodomy might have occurred on stage was only simulated, without the contact required for honest conviction under the statute, a point with which the federal judge sympathized without finding in it any basis for federal interference with state judicial proceedings; and third, that some of the alleged acts of sodomy involved people of different races and therefore, on the basis of *McLaughlin* and *Loving*, were unpunishable. The judge, a practical man, was unmoved. The case was turned away for want of a substantial federal question.[1]

Had the judge accepted the attorney's nimble logic, all pornographic theater might have integrated on the spot to keep the police at bay. But the Supreme Court had earlier shown its unwillingness to come to the aid of interracial sex in the form of public entertainment when it sustained the conviction of Ralph Ginzburg for, among other things, the publication of a magazine containing photographs of a black man and a white woman embracing nude. Justice Douglas, dissenting, quoted critic Dwight Macdonald:

> I suppose if you object to the idea of a Negro and a white person having sex together, then, of course, you would be horrified by it. I don't. From the artistic point of view I thought it was very good. . . .[2]

And another defense witness, the chairman of the Department of Fine Arts at New York University, said:

> I think they are outstandingly beautiful and artistic photographs. . . . The very contrast in the color of the two bodies of course has presented him with certain opportunities that he would not have had with two models of the same color, and he has taken rather extraordinary and very delicate advantage of these contrasts.[3]

Douglas's lonely position aside, federal courts distinguish firmly between individual rights and the presentation of sex as entertainment, and they discourage the exchange of judicial precedent between cases in the two areas.

Domestic relations

More to the point in the thinking of the average judge, *Loving* bears on domestic relations of many kinds not mentioned in the opinion, some with retroactive implications. Under the old dispensation, for example, courts in states which banned mixed marriages might proceed on the assumption that such a marriage had never occurred, sometimes with odd results. Following this nonrecognition principle, a Virginia court once rejected the request of a white woman for a divorce from her Filipino husband, whom she had wed eight years before in New Jersey. No marriage, therefore no divorce, said the court.[4] Virginia would not assist a white woman out of a marriage with a nonwhite despite its official view that such unions were pernicious.

One family tried the very opposite in the wake of *Loving* —to legitimize its miscegenous union in Mississippi retroactively—but without success. Adeline V——, the black mother of two children by an Italian she had considered her husband until his death in 1963, applied for federal social security benefits in 1964 and was turned down because the children were the product of an interracial union, then regarded as a crime rather than a marriage in Mississippi. The federal Social Security Administration denied benefits on the ground that the couple had not represented themselves as husband and wife to the public. Although the evidence is not free of contradiction, it is interesting that the two were together as openly as they were, considering community feelings and the harsh danger of prosecution: when the children were baptized in the Catholic church the parents were fully identified, they attended the high school graduation of one child as husband and wife, and until the status was abolished by the Mississippi legislature in 1956 they lived together as common-law spouses. On the other side, evidence was adduced that she had signed an employment application with her maiden name, that when the couple began living together in 1947 there was an understanding that they would be married in Chicago when he retired, and that in fact she had moved to Illinois to work in a hospital in the late 1950s, although returning frequently to visit V—— and the children and to live with them from 1962 until his death the following year.

Said the federal district court,

> . . . we are unable to assume from the record before
> us that fear of criminal prosecution was the sole reason
> that the parties refrained from holding themselves out
> to the general community as married.[5]

This court's requirements would make it discouragingly difficult for the law to rehabilitate some fugitive marriages
from the time of antimiscegenation law and to bestow the
benefits of legitimacy.

On a question of inheritance a few weeks after *Loving*,
the Supreme Court of Oklahoma was more generous in its
view of a 1939 mixed marriage. Martin D——, a Chickasaw
Indian, died intestate in 1959. His son from his second marriage, to a Chickasaw woman, contended that the offspring
of his first marriage, to a Negro woman, could not inherit a
penny from D—— because his first marriage violated the law
of the state. Citing *Loving*, the court pronounced the miscegenous marriage valid retroactively and allowed the inheritance.[6] In this case the partners to the marriage had lived
together continuously, so there was no question of the actual cohesiveness of the family as in the V—— dispute.

Mississippi demonstrated some flexibility even in pre-*Loving* times on collateral issues such as inheritance, if not on
the issue of mixed marriage itself, which means that the
Loving precedent was not a *sine qua non* for those seeking
mitigation of the effects of antimiscegenation laws there. In
1948, for example, a Mississippi court explained that the
state would recognize an out-of-state miscegenous marriage
to the extent of permitting the survivor, the white husband
of a black woman, to inherit property from her in Mississippi. The two had been residents of Mississippi at one time
and had moved to Illinois to marry. Had they returned together they would have been subject to criminal prosecution
by Mississippi authorities, of course, but the more abstract

union of white man and black property that was requested in this case was held to be unobjectionable.[7] Rather differently, however, a Louisiana decision one year before *Loving* disinherited the natural brothers and sisters of a decedent in favor of having the property pass to the state for want of a proper heir. The court said that miscegenous illegitimates could not be legally acknowledged and therefore could not inherit from one another.[8] The *Loving* decision seems likely to amend this doctrine, perhaps retroactively, if it is challenged in court.

The *Loving* case is also likely to put an end to the power of a state judge to disband a family because adult and child are of different races. In Kentucky, in 1966, a white mother of five children aged six to thirteen divorced her white husband and married a Negro. She tried and failed to convince a federal judge, Henry Brooks, that Jefferson County Court Judge Lyndon Schmid had violated the Constitution of the United States by taking her children from her and placing them in foster homes and juvenile institutions. Judge Schmid said he had acted to preserve the "health, morality and general welfare" of the white children. "Rearing these children in a racially mixed atmosphere per se indoctrinates them with a psychology of inferiority." The mother's lawyers argued that she and the children were suffering a cruel and unusual punishment and a denial of the equal protection of the laws. Judge Brooks found no substantial federal question to warrant intervention.[9]

The couple suffered in other ways. Both lost jobs whenever employers learned of their imperfectly concealed mixed marriage—in one instance the black husband had been observed waiting near a restaurant to drive his wife home from work as a waitress. After Judge Brooks turned the case away, the state compounded its assault on the family by awarding custody of the children to their white father. In a six-page opinion that made no mention of the race

of members of the family, Judge Schmid noted that the natural father had a two-and-a-half story house whereas the
mother lived in a modest apartment in a predominantly
Negro neighborhood, and he dismissed the intelligence that
the father was a professional gambler: "We cannot in this
day and age reach a conclusion that because a parent is a
professional gambler or an amateur gambler that they are
unfit to have custody of their own children." Given the
nearly universal reluctance of American courts to take children from a mother, and particularly from a re-established
home, and turn them over to an unmarried father, gambler
or not, it is plain that racial intermarriage was the sole consideration.[10] If the racial issue were squarely faced now, a
decision such as Judge Schmid's would be vulnerable to attack on constitutional grounds.

In a similar case in Illinois, in 1956, an appellate court
more sensitive than Kentucky's to considerations of racial
equality and the welfare of children reversed a lower court's
award of child custody to the father. Like the Kentucky decision, the lower court's order in Illinois was meant to enforce a degree of racial segregation within the family. But
from that point the facts diverge. In the dispute in Illinois
the children of a divorced mixed couple were given to the
black father, although he had served one year in the penitentiary for rape shortly before the divorce decree. The two
children, said the judge, have "the outstanding basic racial
characteristics of the Negro race . . . and . . . for racial and
religious reasons these children will make a better adjustment to life if allowed to remain identified, reared and educated with the group and basic stock of the plaintiff, their
father." The mother had at the time of divorce agreed to
give up custody, but when she married a white man and
moved into a mixed neighborhood on Chicago's South Side,
she appealed for custody. When the lower court's ruling
against her was contested, the higher court ruled that the

judge had abused his discretion in paying any attention to the racial characteristics of the children, and awarded them to the mother.[11] *Loving* could add nothing to this.

In Texas, the force of the *Loving* precedent was needed to secure a court ruling that a statute which prohibited the adoption of a white person by a Negro was unconstitutional. An El Paso court had denied the request of a Negro to adopt the two illegitimate white daughters of his white wife, even though the four had lived as a family since 1958. The Court of Civil Appeals of Texas in El Paso reversed the decision in November, 1967, allowing the family full legal integrity in the light of *Loving*, which it construed broadly.[12]

A very different marital relationship certain to be radically affected by *Loving* in the few cases in which it occurs, is that of prosecution witness in a criminal proceeding. The accepted principle of law that a husband may not testify against his wife, or a wife against her husband, has been held inapplicable in the case of an unlawfully mixed marriage. In 1942 Frank P——, an Indian, was convicted in an Arizona court of the murder of Sai Han Ong. The testimony of his wife, Ruby, whom he had married three weeks before the killing, was essential to the prosecution. When Frank insisted that she could not be called as a witness without his consent, the court's reply was that the rule that "a descendant of an Indian may not marry a member of the Caucasian race" rendered the marriage null and void. The judge expressed some concern over the difficulty of determining race and hoped the legislature would be more explicit someday, perhaps by defining race by blood percentages, but he had no trouble passing sentence on Frank and giving Ruby her freedom.[13]

Another species of marital revenge has been taken or attempted in a number of instances on record, when one of the partners charged his mate with membership in an inferior race with whom marriage was unlawful. There some-

times followed a particularly harsh and expeditious divorce
in favor of the deceived. In an early case in North Carolina,
a husband contended that his wife had to his surprise
turned out to be a Negro, and the jury agreed that there
was indeed an indication that her great-grandfather had
been black. But the wife appealed, asking instead for a divorce with alimony, for during their courtship, she testified,
she had warned that there were rumors abroad that she had
a strain of Negro blood and that he would be well advised
to think no more of marriage; but he would not be put off.
"After the birth of their little girl," an indignant appellate
court wrote, he "cruelly treated her, would get drunk and
abuse her in the vilest manner, refuse to provide her with
the common necessities of life, and abandoned her and his
own child, and left her without providing her any support.
He left her in a delicate condition, and expressed the wish
that her condition would kill her." The appellate court reversed the decision of the trial court and awarded her the
divorce and the alimony she sought.[14]

The chief justice concurred, and added some thoughts of
his own that must represent one of the clearest victories of
southern gallantry over southern bigotry on record. He believed

> . . . it would be difficult to find a case so void of merit
> as that which the husband presents. Years ago the
> plaintiff married a wife, who, if she had any strain of
> negro blood whatever, was so white he did not suspect
> it till recently, so he states. He does not aver even that
> she deceived him, so she herself must have been un-
> aware of the fact, if it existed. She has borne him chil-
> dren. If he could show fault in her conduct in any way,
> it is to be presumed that in these days of easy divorce
> he would have sued on that ground. His divorced wife

might in some circumstances have been still entitled to alimony and dower.

The plaintiff by earnest solicitation persuaded the defendant to become his wife in the days of her youth and beauty. She has borne his children. Now, that youth has fled and household drudgery and childbearing have taken the sparkle from her eyes, and deprived her form of its symmetry, he seeks to get rid of her, not only without fault alleged against her, but in a method that will not only deprive her of any support while he lives by alimony, or by dower after his death, but which would consign her to the association of the colored race, which he so affects to despise. The law may not permit him thus to bastardize his own innocent children, . . . but he would brand them for all time by the judgment of a court as negroes—a fate which their white skin will make doubly humiliating to them. If, indeed, the plaintiff had discovered any minute strain of colored origin after the youth of his wife has been worn away for his pleasure and in his service, justice and generosity dictated that he keep to himself that of which the public was unaware, or, if the knowledge had become public and was disagreeable, the plaintiff, if possessed of any sentiment of manhood, would have shielded his wife and children by removing to another locality or to a state where the fact, if known, would not be deemed a stigma. Certainly of all men he should have welcomed the verdict that decided his wife and children are white.

. . . He deems it perdition for himself to associate with those possessing the slightest suspicion of negro blood, but strains every effort to consign the wife of his bosom and the innocent children of his own loins to poverty and to the infamy that he depicts. The jury did not find with him, and he has no reason to ask any court to aid him in such a purpose.[15]

In Arizona a few years later, Joe K—— had better fortune in a similar action against his wife, Mayellen, to whom he had been married many years. Alleging that he was a Caucasian with an Irish father and a mother of Mexican extraction, Joe charged in court that Mayellen was black. She retorted that his mother had a trace of Indian blood, which if true would have maintained the marriage because Arizona law at the time permitted intermarriage among those with non-Caucasian ancestry. The court disagreed with her. She then argued that the Arizona miscegenation law was unconstitutional. Again the court disagreed. The marriage was annulled.[16] One of the implications of *Loving* is that disenchanted husbands and wives will have to confine their public complaints about their spouses to nonracial categories such as cruelty, desertion, and adultery.

The wider implications of *Loving* in the law of domestic relations are a matter of speculation. Father Drinan, then dean of the Boston College School of Law, wrote not long ago that the decision may lead to a general relaxation of the rules governing the right to marry. Should there even be marriage "licenses," he wondered, or merely registration of prospective partners who have satisfied themselves of their qualifications for matrimony? *Loving* hints, but does not say, that any statutory restraint on the freedom to marry must be based on potential harm to the offspring of the marriage or on some clear moral or medical ground. Consanguinity laws forbidding intermarriage among people who are distantly related might be questioned for want of scientific foundation.[17]

Social experiments

Even beyond Father Drinan's musings lies the question of the legitimacy of homosexual and polygamous marriages. As homosexual couples apply for licenses and force courts to consider their demands, conflicting rulings are certain to put pressure on the federal courts to apply the rationale of *Loving*. In Louisville, Kentucky, for example, two women tried to secure a marriage license from the county clerk, coming up against an unyielding county attorney. In Minnesota, the courts denied a license to two male applicants.[18] Another development in the law affirms the strength of the tradition of heterosexuality: a New York judge recently granted a divorce to a Navy veteran who had undergone surgery to become a woman. A marriage of two women, said the judge, who both in his opinion seem to have become the mother of the child, is no marriage.[19] The Vatican has given attention to the increasing popularity of formal homosexual unions, labelling them "marriages against nature" in its official newspaper:

> Neither scientific nor juridical progress will be able to modify the nature of things, changing the establishment of marriage which has as protagonists two people of different sex.

The statement concluded:

> Attempts to give to marriage new contents and aspects are simple moral aberrations which cannot be approved either by the human conscience or, especially, by the Christian conscience.[20]

But if the Catholic church does not bend, the law may.

The rural and urban communes which have been popular in the United States since the 1960s present numerous problems touching the limits of public tolerance and the law's adaptability. Communal living in its various forms seems to pose a threat to hoary traditions of monogamous marriage, responsibility for the care of infants, privacy, and sexual decency, and at times to the positive laws of conscription, narcotics, the delinquency of minors, public welfare, sanitation, and residential zoning as well. Rural settlements of the kind that flourished in northern New Mexico around 1969 are now giving way to more substantial urban communes, according to all reports—a trend that promises increasing litigation.

As long as communes were rustic, community disapproval could be expressed informally—ostracism in town, vigilante raids at home, sniping, and assault. One commune by the name of Oz survived only four months of harassment by local citizens and police.[21] The three dozen members of the Oz "family" had come from California to a rude farmhouse and 130 acres of land in rural Pennsylvania. Trouble soon came to Oz: angry parents from the vicinity arrived to look for runaway teenagers, and health officials broadcast stern warnings of hepatitis on the radio. Spicy rumors circulated, and local interest in the farm grew accordingly, culminating in shootings, arson, and the attempted abduction of an Oz girl. Shortly after a protest meeting in town, state police raided the commune and arrested the members under an 1860 law punishing anyone who "keeps and maintains a common, ill-governed and disorderly house" encouraging "idleness, gaming, drinking, or misbehavior to the common nuisance or disturbance of the neighborhood and orderly citizens. . . ." Another complaint alleged the corruption of the morals of a sixteen-year-old girl, and then a small child was taken from its mother by authorities with the explanation that life in the Oz family was substandard in health and morals—as indicated by thick flies and nudity, among other things. Police tacked a court order to the farmhouse forbidding the use of the premises for "fornication, assignation, and lewdness," and soon, under an agreement with the district attorney, the Oz family left town to escape trial. Their empty farmhouse was burned to the ground a few days later.

A peaceful group with deviant ways that excited disgust and wrath in conventional minds, the family disappeared rather than invite eventual destruction by a tightly knit moral community. An appeal to higher courts for protection or redefinition of the law in their favor was not feasible.

Lately an estimated two or three thousand communes have been formed in cities, often without characteristics associated with hippie culture. Herbert Otto has found an interesting variety in his studies, including what he calls the craft commune, the spiritual-mystical, the denominational, the church-sponsored, the political, the art commune, the service commune, the homosexual, and the group-marriage commune.[22] Many are more purposeful and sophisticated than Oz, more adept at the art of public relations or urban anonymity in the avoidance of friction with neighbors and officials. Members are old, young, or mixed, sometimes professionals, and when challenged they may be expected to press their claims for legal immunity plus a share of the tax and welfare benefits enjoyed by traditional families. Perhaps as much as a fifth of the population may experiment with communal alternatives to the nuclear family, Otto predicts. If so, the laws of the states will be severely strained and the state and federal courts will be under mounting pressure from litigants and assisting organizations for a rereading of the Constitution to guarantee not only a choice of marital partner, in the *Loving* tradition, but of marital configuration too. The courts will have the option of falling back on the established rule that the larger community may require

monogamy of all,[23] or enlarging the libertarian implications
of *Loving* into a broad defense of deviance from community
norms in family living. Logically, it would be simple to add
to the choice of race, in *Loving,* the choices of number, of
sex, and of duration.

For some time the taboos involved in these social experi-
ments will induce public officials and judges to reiterate old
constraints. The response of a federal court in California to
the complaints of the Palo Alto Tenants Union in December
1970 is a case in point. Judge Albert Wollenberg firmly
denied the request of two "families" of legally unrelated
young people for protection from what they described as
harassment in the guise of enforcement of zoning regulations by Palo Alto city officials.[24] Like many municipalities,
Palo Alto reserves some areas for single-family residences,
closely defining a family as "one person living alone, or two
or more persons related by blood, marriage, or legal adoption, or a group not exceeding four persons living as a single
housekeeping unit"—a bar to communal living unless the
members choose mass adoption proceedings as a way
around the literal requirements of the ordinance.

With the help of the Legal Aid Society of San Mateo
County, the commune contended that a number of provisions of the United States Constitution had been violated
when Palo Alto's laws were brought to bear on them: freedom of association and the rights of privacy in the Bill of
Rights and the equal protection guarantee of the Fourteenth Amendment.

Judge Wollenberg not only refused to adopt an enlarged
view of the Constitution; he turned the important precedent
of *Griswold* v. *Connecticut* [25] against those who had raised
it, as another judge someday may employ *Loving* v. *Virginia.* Far from being a general authorization of experimen-
tation in new forms of family association, in Wollenberg's
opinion, *Griswold's* strictures on official interference with
birth control were a defense of privacy in "bilateral" mar-

riage specifically, and no more. He quoted the wistful words
of a newly remarried Justice Douglas:

> Marriage is a coming together for better or for
> worse, hopefully enduring, and intimate to the degree
> of being sacred. It is an association that promotes a
> way of life, not causes; a harmony in living, not politi-
> cal faiths; a bilateral loyalty. . . .

Judge Wollenberg felt that Palo Alto's ordinance was not
unreasonable, and that it did not impinge on a "fundamental interest" requiring the special protection of the Constitution:

> . . . there is a long recognized value in the tradi-
> tional family relationship which does not attach to the
> "voluntary family." The traditional family is an institu-
> tion reinforced by biological and legal ties which are
> difficult, or impossible, to sunder. It plays a role in ed-
> ucating and nourishing the young which, far from
> being "voluntary," is often compulsory. Finally, it has
> been a means, for uncounted millenia, of satisfying the
> deepest emotional and physical needs of human
> beings. A zoning law which divided or totally excluded
> traditional families would indeed be "suspect."
>
> The communal living groups represented by plain-
> tiffs share few of the above characteristics. They are
> voluntary, with fluctuating memberships who have no
> legal obligations of support or cohabitation. They are
> in no way subject to the State's vast body of domestic
> relations law. They do not have the biological links
> which characterize most families. Emotional ties be-
> tween commune members may exist, but this is true of
> members of many groups. Plaintiffs are unquestionably
> sincere in seeking to devise and test new life-styles, but
> the communes they have formed are legally indistin-
> guishable from such traditional living groups as reli-

gious communities and residence clubs. The right to form such groups may be constitutionally protected, but the right to insist that these groups live under the same roof, in any part of the city they choose, is not.

Loving v. *Virginia* may sooner or later be raised in suits questioning the primacy of the traditional family. It will be interesting to see whether it is wielded most successfully by those who favor innovation or by the defenders of the *status quo*.

Speculations aside, the *Loving* case did have a perceptible impact in two places. In the predominantly black District of Columbia the superintendent of schools ordered offending passages cut from an eleventh grade health text. School staff members manned razor blades in the schools throughout the city. The book *Personal Adjustment, Marriage and Family Living*, had been found to say in a passage on racial mixing that ". . . acceptance in the community may be difficult or impossible for the marriage partners and their children to obtain." And, "Interracial marriages may not be illegal but they are unwise." [26] The censoring was reminiscent of the removal of Garth Williams's children's picture book, *The Rabbits' Wedding*, from southern library and school shelves not long after its publication in 1958, when its supposed moral was divined. Williams, with abundant charm, tells the story of a little white rabbit and a little black rabbit who romp and play together and fall deeply in love, marry, and live happily ever after among the daisies and the dandelions. The book was thought to be rather too suggestive for first graders and was taken away in the interest of racial harmony.

And in Caroline County, the home of the Lovings, the sheriff and commonwealth attorney who had prosecuted them were both defeated in the next election.[27]

Notes

Chapter 1

1. 388 U.S. 1 (1967).
2. "Miscegenation," from the Latin *miscere* (mix) and *genus* (race), was coined by the authors of an anonymous pamphlet, *Miscegenation: The Theory of the Blending of the Races,* published in 1864, in reality an attempt by Democrats David Croly and George Wakeman to attribute favorable views on racial mixing to the Republicans and thereby aid the Democratic candidate for president.
3. Simeon Booker, "The Couple That Rocked the Courts," *Ebony,* September 1967, p. 78; *Washington Post,* June 13, 1967.
4. *Washington Post,* June 13, 1967.
5. American Civil Liberties Union, *Feature Press Service,* March 15, 1965.
6. 347 U.S. 537 (1954).
7. 348 U.S. 888 (1954).
8. 350 U.S. 891 and 985 (1956).
9. Walter F. Murphy, *Elements of Judicial Strategy* (Chicago: University of Chicago Press, 1964), p. 193.
10. 379 U.S. 184 (1964).
11. *Doremus* v. *Board of Education,* 342 U.S. 429 (1952); *Engel* v. *Vitale,* 370 U.S. 421 (1962); *Murray* v. *Curlett,* 374 U.S. 203 (1963).
12. U.S., Congress, Senate, Committee on the Judiciary, *The Nomination of Thurgood Marshall to the Supreme Court,* 90th Cong., 1st sess., 1967, p. 175.
13. 388 U.S. 307 (1967).
14. Murphy, *Judicial Strategy,* p. 195.

Chapter 2

1. *Time,* April 6, 1970, p. 94.
2. George De Vos, "The Psychology of Purity and Pollution as Related

to Social Self-Identity and Caste," in *Caste and Race: Comparative Approaches,* ed. Anthony de Reuck and Julie Knight (Boston: Little, Brown & Co., 1967), p. 298.

3. G. W. Allport, *The Nature of Prejudice* (Cambridge, Mass.: Addison-Wesley, 1954), p. 374.

4. E. J. B. Rose, *Colour and Citizenship* (London: Oxford University Press, 1969), pp. 448–49.

5. Helen V. McLean, "Psychoanalytic Factors in Racial Relations," *Annals* 144 (1946): 65.

6. John Dollard, *Caste and Class in a Southern Town* (New Haven: Yale University Press, 1937), p. 170 n. 21.

7. De Vos, "Psychology of Purity," p. 66.

8. W. J. Cash, *The Mind of the South* (New York: Alfred A. Knopf, Inc., 1941), p. 86.

9. Dollard, *Caste and Class,* p. 136 n. 4.

10. T. F. Pettigrew, "Personality and Sociocultural Factors in Intergroup Attitudes," *Conflict Resolution* 2 (1958): 38.

11. Ibid., p. 30.

12. E. T. Prothro, "Ethnocentrism and Anti-Negro Attitudes in the Deep South," *Journal of Abnormal and Social Psychology* 47 (1952): 105–8.

13. T. F. Pettigrew, "Social Psychology and Desegregation Research," *American Psychologist* 16 (1961): 109; but compare R. W. Hites and E. P. Kellog, "The F and Social Maturity Scales in Relation to Racial Attitudes in a Deep South Sample," *Journal of Social Psychology* 62 (1964): 189.

14. *Gallup Political Index,* Report No. 18, November-December 1966, pp. 19–21.

15. De Vos, "Psychology of Purity," p. 302.

16. H. C. Kelman and Janet Barclay, "The F Scale as a Measure of Breadth of Perspective," *Journal of Abnormal and Social Psychology* 67 (1963): 609.

17. T. W. Adorno et al., *The Authoritarian Personality* (New York: Harper, 1950), pp. 366–67 and 455.

18. Allport, *Nature of Prejudice,* pp. 398–99.

19. Ibid., p. 348.

20. *New York Times,* January 23, 1970, p. 16.

21. Quoted in John H. Wilharm, Jr., "Racial Intermarriage–A Constitutional Problem," *Western Reserve Law Review* 11 (1959): 93.

22. C. U. Smith and J. W. Prothro, "Ethnic Differences in the Authoritarian Personality," *Social Forces* 35 (1957): 336.

23. H. Hendin, "Black Suicide," *Archives of General Psychiatry* 21 (1969): 407–22.

24. *U. S. News and World Report,* November 18, 1963, p. 85.

25. J. D. Barber, *The Lawmakers* (New Haven: Yale University Press, 1965).

26. *New York Times,* November 7, 1965, p. 73.

27. Sister Annella Lynn, *Interracial Marriages in Washington, D. C., 1940–1947* (Washington, D. C.: Catholic University of America Press, 1953), pp. 49 ff.

28. Albert I. Gordon, *Intermarriage: Interfaith, Interracial, Interethnic* (Boston: Beacon Press, 1964), pp. 60 ff.

29. *New York Times*, October 19, 1970, p. 26. Here and elsewhere I have abbreviated last names in the interest of privacy for the victims of race law. In each instance the name is accessible to scholars who care to find the article or court decision cited.

30. *New York Times*, November 7, 1965, p. 73.

Chapter 3

1. *New York Times*, September 12, 1963, p. 30.

2. Quoted in Milton Mayer, "The Issue is Miscegenation," *Progressive*, September, 1959, p. 8.

3. Paul M. Angle, ed., *Created Equal: The Complete Lincoln-Douglas Debates of 1858* (Chicago: University of Chicago Press, 1959), pp. 235–36.

4. *Othello*, act 1, sc. 1, lines 88–89 and 108–14.

5. Helen B. Shaffer, "Mixed Marriage," *Editorial Research Reports* (1961): 381.

6. The Staff of Social Science I of the College of the University of Chicago, eds., *The People Shall Judge* (Chicago: University of Chicago Press, 1949), 1:784–87.

7. W. C. Brann, *Brann the Iconoclast* (Waco, Texas: Brann Publishing Co., 1898), 1:24–29.

8. Theodore Bilbo, *Take Your Choice* (Poplarville, Mississippi: Dream House Publishing Co., 1947), p. 292.

9. U.S., Congress, House, Committee on Un-American Activities, *Hearings*, 89th Cong., 2d sess., 1966, Pt. 3, p. 2389.

10. U.S., Congress, House, Committee on Un-American Activities, *Report*, 90th Cong., 1st sess., 1967, H. Doc. 377, p. 184.

11. House, Un-American Activities, *Hearings*, 89th Cong., 2d sess., 1966, Pt. 4, pp. 2920–21.

12. *New York Times*, July 11, 1965, p. 46.

13. Letter to the editor from Mississippi, *Ebony*, August, 1965, p. 8.

14. U.S., Congress, House, *Congressional Record*, 98th Cong., 1st sess., March 30, 1965, pp. 6333–34.

15. Ibid., April 27, 1965, pp. 8595–97.

16. Herbert Ravenal Sass, "Mixed Schools and Mixed Blood," *Atlantic Monthly*, November 1956, p. 48. Other passages quoted below are from pages 46 and 47.

17. See *New York Times*, June 12, 1965, p. 1, and June 17, 1967, p. 26,

154   *Notes*

Ebony, October 1965, pp. 66–75, and *Albuquerque Journal,* October 18, 1970, for examples.

18. *New York Times,* November 10, 1968, p. 123.
19. *Gallup Opinion Index,* Report No. 631, September 1970, p. 27.
20. William Brink and Louis Harris, *Black and White* (New York: Simon & Schuster, 1966), p. 132.
21. *Polls,* Summer 1965, I: 75.
22. *Borders* v. *Rippy,* 184 F. Supp. 402, 404 (1960).
23. Ibid., 405–6.
24. Ibid., 409–10.
25. Ibid., 415–17.
26. *Dred Scott* v. *Sandford,* 60 U.S. (19 How.) 393, 409 (1857).
27. "*Philadelphia & West Chester R. R. Co.* v. *Miles,*" *American Law Review,* n.d., cited in *State* v. *Gibson,* 10 Am. Rep. 42 (1871).
28. *Scott* v. *State,* 39 Ga. 321, 324–26.
29. *State* v. *Bell,* 32 Am. Rep. 549 (1872).
30. *Hayes* v. *Crutcher,* 108 F. Supp. 582, 585 (1952).
31. *Florida* ex rel. *Hawkins* v. *Board of Control,* 83 So.2d 20, 27–28 (1955).
32. *Borders* v. *Rippy,* 407.
33. Ibid., 408.
34. Ibid., 413–14.
35. Ibid., 415.
36. Ibid., 409.
37. Victor S. Navasky, "The Government and Martin Luther King," *Atlantic,* November 1970, pp. 48 and 52.
38. Mayer, "Miscegenation," p. 11; Ashley Montagu, "The Myth of Blood," *Psychiatry* 6 (1943): 15–19.
39. *Public Opinion Quarterly* 10 (Winter 1946–1947): 624.
40. Matas, "Surgical Peculiarities of the Negro," *Transactions of the American Surgical Association* 4 (1896), cited in student note, "Constitutionality of Anti-Miscegenation Statutes," *Yale Law Journal* (February, 1949), p. 474, n. 12.
41. W. A. Dixon, "The Morbid Proclivities and Retrogressive Tendencies in the Offspring of Mulattoes," *Journal of the American Medical Association* 20 (1893), No. 1, January 7, unpaged.
42. Ashley Montagu, *Man's Most Dangerous Myth: The Fallacy of Race* (Cleveland: World Publishing Co., 1964), pp. 193, 196–97, 201, and 214.
43. Ibid., pp. 187–91. Also see C. Stern, *Principles of Human Genetics* (San Francisco: W. H. Freeman, 1949), pp. 563–79.
44. Montagu, *Dangerous Myth,* pp. 188 and 191.
45. N. A. Barnicot, "Taxonomy and Variations in Modern Man," in *The Concept of Race,* ed. Ashley Montagu (New York: Free Press of Glencoe, 1964), pp. 194–95.
46. Group for the Advancement of Psychiatry, Report No. 37 (New York: Committee on Social Issues, 1957), pp. 26–30.

47. Ibid., p. 92.

48. Carleton Putnam, *Race and Reason* (Washington, D. C.: Public Affairs Press, 1961), p. 67. In a sequel, *Race and Reality* (Washington, D. C.: Public Affairs Press, 1967), Putnam tells his story of liberal and scientific resistance and indifference to his views on race.

49. Putnam, *Race and Reason*, p. 7.

50. *New York Times*, January 15, 1965, p. 42.

51. *New York Times*, February 20, 1965, p. 24.

52. *New York Times*, January 2, 1965, p. 18.

53. *U. S. News and World Report*, November 18, 1963, pp. 92–93.

54. Margaret Mead, "Introductory Remarks," in *Science and the Concept of Race*, eds. Margaret Mead et al. (New York: Columbia University Press, 1968), p. 3.

55. Ibid., Pt. 3.

56. Ibid., pp. 5, 7, 78, and 103. Montagu's views are found in *Dangerous Myth*, pp. 228 and 232.

57. *New York Times*, April 29, 1971, p. 24.

58. *New York Times*, October 14, 1965, p. 30.

59. *New York Times*, May 22, 1965, p. 20. See Joseph R. Washington, Jr., *Marriage in Black and White* (Boston: Beacon Press, 1970), ch. 6, for a more recent selection of religious views.

60. *New York Times*, May 22, 1965, p. 20.

61. *New York Times*, September 29, 1966, p. 29.

62. For example, Herbert McCloskey, "Consensus and Ideology in American Politics," *American Political Science Review* 58 (1964): 361–82.

Chapter 4

1. *New York Times*, March 13, 1966, sec. 4, p. 12.

2. Arizona, California, Colorado, Idaho, Indiana, Maryland, Michigan, Montana, Nebraska, Nevada, North Dakota, Oregon, South Dakota, Utah, and Wyoming.

3. U. S., Supreme Court, *Records and Briefs* in the case of *Loving v. Virginia*, Brief for Appellants, pp. 17–23.

4. *Records and Briefs*, Jurisdictional Statement, pp. 3 ff.

5. Ibid.

6. *Records and Briefs*, Brief for Appellants, pp. 21–23.

7. *City of Richmond v. Deans*, 37 F.2d 712 (1930).

8. George E. Simpson and J. Milton Yinger, *Racial and Cultural Minorities*, rev. ed. (New York: Harper, 1958), p. 561.

9. *Washington Post*, December 25 and 29, 1948 and January 1, 1949.

10. *New York Times*, June 4, 1970, p. 20.

11. *G—— v. State*, 50 So.2d 797 (1951).

12. *U. S. News and World Report*, October 26, 1964, p. 10.

156   *Notes*

13. William D. Zabel, "Interracial Marriage and the Law," *Atlantic Monthly,* October 1965, p. 77.
14. *New York Times,* November 4, 1962, p. 43.
15. *Weaver* v. *State,* 116 So. 893 (1928).
16. Ibid.
17. *R——* v. *State,* 107 So.2d 728 (1958).
18. Zabel, "Interracial Marriage," p. 77.
19. Ibid.
20. Irving G. Tragen, "Statutory Prohibitions Against Interracial Marriage," *California Law Review* 32 (1948): 276–77.
21. *Norman* v. *Norman,* 54 Pac. 143 (1898).
22. *New York Times,* September 4, 1963, p. 27.
23. *Newsweek,* September 16, 1963, pp. 26–27.
24. *New York Times,* September 3, 1963, p. 27.
25. Ibid.
26. *New York Times,* September 4, 1963, p. 27.
27. *New York Times,* September 8, 1963, sec. 4, p. 11.
28. *New York Times,* July 11, 1965, p. 49.
29. *New York Times,* February 12, 1966, p. 56, and *Newsweek,* February 25, 1966, p. 25.
30. *New York Times,* February 14, 1964, p. 33.
31. Lee M. Miller, untitled student note, *Maryland Law Review* 25 (1965): 48.
32. *New York Times,* March 9, 1966, p. 8, and March 23, 1966, p. 30.
33. *New York Times,* March 29, 1966, p. 29.
34. *Maryland Code Annotated,* Art. 27, sec. 416.
35. Simeon Booker, "The Couple That Rocked the Courts," *Ebony,* September 1967, pp. 78–80.
36. Ibid.
37. *Records and Briefs,* Transcript of Record, p. 2. The details of the *Loving* case described in the following pages are from the same source and are not separately cited.
38. American Civil Liberties Union, *Feature Press Service,* June 13, 1966.
39. Gunnar Myrdal, *An American Dilemma* (New York: Harper, 1944), pp. 60–62.
40. *U. S. News and World Report,* September 2, 1963, p. 9.
41. See Henry J. Abraham, *The Judicial Process,* 2d ed. (New York: Oxford University Press, 1968), pp. 236–40.

Chapter 5

1. *Dred Scott* v. *Sandford,* 60 U.S. (19 How.) 393, 409 (1857).
2. 16 Wall. 36 (1873).

3. *State* v. *Gibson*, 10 Am. Rep. 42, 45–54 (1871).
4. 163 U.S. 537 (1896).
5. 347 U.S. 438 (1954).
6. *Civil Rights Cases*, 109 U.S. 3 (1883).
7. *State* v. *Brown*, 108 So.2d 233, 234 (1959).
8. 198 P.2d 17 (1948).
9. Ibid.
10. Ibid.
11. 341 U.S. 494 (1951); 372 U.S. 335 (1963).
12. 348 U.S. 888; 350 U.S. 891 and 985; 379 U.S. 184.
13. U. S., Supreme Court, *Records and Briefs* in the case of *McLaughlin* v. *Florida*, Transcript of Record, *passim*. Details of the *McLaughlin* case described below are drawn from the *Records and Briefs* and are not cited separately.
14. *New York Times*, November 22, 1964, sec. 6, p. 30.
15. *New York Times*, Ocotber 15, 1964, p. 34.
16. *New Republic*, May 30, 1964, pp. 4–5.
17. "The Supreme Court, 1964 Term," *Harvard Law Review* 79 (1965): 168.
18. Lee M. Miller, untitled student note, *Maryland Law Review* 25 (1965): 48.
19. George M. Fleming, student note on *McLaughlin* v. *Florida*, *Mississippi Law Journal* 37 (1965): 167.
20. 348 U.S. 888 (1954).

Chapter 6

1. See Stephen L. Wasby, *The Impact of the United States Supreme Court: Some Perspectives* (Homewood, Ill.: Dorsey Press, 1970).
2. John M. Pittman, student note on *Loving* v. *Virginia*, *Arkansas Law Review* 21 (1967): 439.
3. Sidney L. Moore, student note on *Loving* v. *Virginia*, *Mercer Law Review* 19 (1968): 257.
4. John H. Burma, "Interethnic Marriage in Los Angeles, 1948–1959," *Social Forces* 42 (1963): 157.
5. *Davis* v. *Gately*, 269 F. Supp. 996 (1967); *New York Times*, January 25, 1968, p. 5 and February 2, 1968, p. 4.
6. *Van Hook* v. *Blanton*, 206 So.2d 210 (1968); *New York Times*, January 25, 1968, p. 5 and February 2, 1968, p. 4.
7. *New York Times*, July 11, 1967, p. 23.
8. *New York Times*, August 12, 1967, p. 31.
9. *New York Times*, July 22, 1967, p. 11.
10. *New York Times*, September 30, 1967, p. 28, and October 7, 1967, p. 58.

11. *New York Times*, January 12, 1968, p. 32, and January 14, 1968, p. 62.

12. *New York Times*, October 19, 1970, p. 26.

13. *New York Times*, August 3, 1970, p. 1, *New York Times*, April 16, 1972, p. 18.

14. *New York Times*, December 4, 1970, p. 1.

15. *New York Times*, December 9, 1970, p. 40, *Albuquerque Journal*, December 11, 1970, and *New York Times*, February 13, 1972, p. 62.

16. *Moore* v. *Tangipahoa Parish School Board*, 304 F. Supp. 244 (1969); Robert B. Barnett, "The Constitutionality of Sex Separation in School Desegregation Plans," *University of Chicago Law Review* 37 (1970): 296; *New York Times*, June 4, 1970, p. 20.

17. William Brink and Louis Harris, *Black and White*, (New York: Simon & Schuster, 1966), p. 132.

18. *New York Times*, September 10, 1970, p. 22.

19. *Polls*, Winter 1967, 3: 77.

20. *Polls*, Summer 1965, 1: 75; *New York Times*, September 10, 1970, p. 22.

21. Albert I. Gordon, *Intermarriage: Interfaith, Interracial, Interethnic* (Boston: Beacon Press, 1964), p. 20.

22. Brink and Harris, *Black and White*, p. 109.

23. American Institute of Public Opinion, Poll No. 764, June, 1968. I am indebted to George E. Triplett for assistance in the analysis of this poll and to the University of New Mexico for a grant to obtain the full returns from the Roper Public Opinion Research Center at Williams College.

24. *Public Opinion Quarterly* 7 (Spring 1943): 167. 95.0, 92.8, and 91.6 percent, respectively, refused to consider marriage to a Negro.

25. Brink and Harris, *Black and White*, p. 133; Gordon, *Intermarriage*, p. 20.

26. AIPO Poll No. 764.

27. *New York Times*, September 10, 1970, p. 22.

28. *New York Times*, November 10, 1968, p. 123.

29. *New York Times*, August 21, 1964, p. 20.

30. Quoted in Andrew D. Weinberger, "A Reappraisal of the Constitutionality of Miscegenation Statutes," *Cornell Law Quarterly* 42 (1957): 211.

31. *New York Times*, April 21, 1965, p. 28.

32. *U. S. News and World Report*, November 18, 1963, p. 88.

33. *New York Times*, May 25, 1964, p. 25.

34. *New York Times*, December 7, 1969, p. 82.

35. *Boston Globe*, March 11, 1965, cited in David M. Heer, "Negro-White Marriage in the United States," *Journal of Marriage and the Family* 28 (1966): 262.

36. *New York Times*, June 9, 1968, sec. 6, p. 44.

37. Paul B. Sheatsley, "White Attitudes Toward the Negro," *Daedalus* 95 (Winter 1966): 231.

38. W. E. B. DuBois, *Black Reconstruction in America* (New York: S. A. Russell, 1935), p. 35.
39. Carter G. Woodson, "The Beginnings of the Miscegenation of the Whites and Blacks," *Journal of Negro History* 3 (1918): 340.
40. Ibid., p. 342.
41. DuBois, *Black Reconstruction*, p. 3.
42. *U. S. News and World Report*, November 18, 1963, pp. 85 and 91.
43. Allison Davis, Burleigh Gardner, and Mary Gardner, *Deep South* (Chicago: University of Chicago Press, 1941), pp. 32–39.
44. *Newsweek*, October 2, 1967, pp. 23–24.
45. Sister Annella Lynn, *Interracial Marriages in Washington, D. C., 1940--1947* (Washington, D. C.: Catholic University of America Press, 1953), pp. 6–7; Robert K. Merton, "Intermarriage and the Social Structure," *Psychiatry* 4 (1941): 366.
46. Cited in Helen B. Shaffer, "Mixed Marriage," *Editorial Research Reports* (1961): 381.
47. Lynn, *Interracial Marriages*, p. 63.
48. Larry D. Barnett, "Research on International and Interracial Marriage," *Marriage and Family Living* 25 (1963): 105–7.
49. John H. Burma, "Interethnic Marriage in Los Angeles, 1948–1959," *Social Forces* 42 (1963): 156.
50. Heer, "Negro-White Marriage," pp. 262–267; *New York Times*, October 18, 1963, p. 1.
51. *New York Times*, June 9, 1968, sec. 6, p. 44.
52. *United States Census*, 1960, Vol. PC(2)–4E: *Marital Status*, p. 160.
53. Lynn, *Interracial Marriages*, pp. 5 and 24.
54. W. E. B. DuBois, *The Gift of Black Folk* (Boston: Stratford, 1924), pp. 268–69.
55. *U. S. News and World Report*, November 18, 1963, p. 87; *New York Times*, November 7, 1965, p. 73; George E. Simpson and J. Milton Yinger, *Racial and Cultural Minorities*, rev. ed. (New York: Harper, 1958), p. 564, n. 79.
56. Joseph Golden, "Characteristics of the Negro-White Intermarried in Philadelphia," *American Sociological Review* 18 (1953): 178.
57. Sidney M. Morton, "Interracial Births in Baltimore, 1950–1964," *Public Health Reports*, 81, no. 11 (1966): 967–71.
58. California, Department of Public Health, *Marriage by Race of Bride and Groom, California, 1955, 1957–1959*, mimeo, n. d.
59. Louis Wirth and Herbert Goldhamer, "The Hybrid and the Problem of Miscegenation," in *Characteristics of the American Negro*, ed. Otto Klineberg (New York: Harper, 1944), p. 281.
60. 1960 *Census*, p. 160.
61. Ibid.
62. Heer, "Negro-White Marriage," p. 267.
63. Figures reported by the Public Health Service, U. S. Department of

Health, Education, and Welfare, indicate a clear and continuing preponderance of black grooms and white brides in mixed marriages. The states separately listed are nonsouthern and the national sample from the "marriage-registration area" underrepresents the South. *Notes on Interracial Marriage*, mimeo, n. d.; *Marriage Statistics Analysis: United States, 1963* (Washington, D. C., 1968).

64. Virginia, Department of Health, *Number of Marriages by Race of Bride and Groom, Virginia, 1967 and 1968*, mimeo, n. d.

65. 1960 *Census*, p. 171.

66. Pierre L. van den Berghe, "Hypergamy, Hypergenation, and Miscegenation," *Human Relations* 13 (1960): 83–89.

67. Shaffer, "Mixed Marriage," p. 316.

68. Merton, "Intermarriage," p. 372.

69. Barnett, "International and Interracial Marriage," pp. 105–7; Todd H. Pavela, "An Exploratory Study of Negro-White Intermarriage in Indiana," *Journal of Marriage and the Family* 26 (1964): 209–11.

70. Golden, "Intermarried in Philadelphia," p. 179; *New York Times*, June 9, 1968, sec. 6, p. 44.

71. Clotye M. Larsson, ed., *Marriage Across the Color Line* (Chicago: Johnson, 1965), pp. 58 ff. and 120.

72. Pavela, "Intermarriage in Indiana," p. 211.

73. Lynn, *Interracial Marriages*, p. 46.

74. *New York Times*, December 19, 1964, p. 18.

75. *New York Times*, July 15, 1968, p. 23.

76. *Swann* v. *Charlotte-Mecklenburg Board of Education*, 402 U.S. 1 (1971).

77. Lynn, *Interracial Marriages*, p. 32.

78. *Report of the National Advisory Commission on Civil Disorders* (New York: Bantam, 1968), pp. 246–47.

79. *New York Times*, September 28, 1970, p. 1.

80. Milton L. Barron, "Research on Intermarriage: A Survey of Accomplishments and Prospects," *American Journal of Sociology* 57 (1951): 250.

81. Pavela, "Intermarriage in Indiana," passim.

82. Randall Risdon, "A Study of Intermarriages Based on Data for Los Angeles County," *Sociology and Social Research* 39 (1954): 93.

83. John H. Burma, "Research Note on the Measurement of Interracial Marriage," *American Journal of Sociology* 57 (1952): 587–89.

Chapter 7

1. *Raphael* v. *Hogan*, 305 F. Supp. 749 (1969).
2. *Ginzburg* v. *United States*, 383 U.S. 463, 487 (1966).
3. Ibid., 487–88.

4. Hans J. Massaquoi, "Would You Want Your Daughter To Marry One?" *Ebony*, August 1965, p. 86.

5. *V—— v. Gardner*, 290 F. Supp. 200, 206 (1968).

6. *D—— v. Reaves*, 434 P.2d 295 (1967).

7. *Miller v. Luchs*, 36 So.2d 140 (1948).

8. *Hibbert v. Mudd*, 187 So.2d 503 (1966).

9. *New York Times*, March 25, 1966, p. 29, March 26, 1966, p. 30, and July 8, 1966, p. 12.

10. *New York Times*, July 8, 1966, p. 12.

11. *F—— v. F——*, 133 N.E.2d 532 (1956).

12. *In re G——*, 424 S.W.2d 656 (1967).

13. *State v. P——*, 121 P.2d 882 (1942).

14. *F—— v. F——*, 69 S.E. 60 (1910).

15. Ibid., 62–63.

16. *K—— v. K——*, 206 Pac. 405 (1922).

17. Robert F. Drinan, S. J., "The Loving Decision and the Freedom to Marry," *Ohio State Law Journal* 29 (1968): 376.

18. *Time*, November 1, 1971, p. 98.

19. *New York Times*, October 8, 1970, p. 62.

20. *Albuquerque Journal*, July 30, 1970.

21. The story of Oz is drawn from Robert Houriet, "Life and Death of a Commune Called Oz," *New York Times*, February 16, 1969, sec. 6, p. 30.

22. Herbert Otto, "Communes: The Alternative Life-Style," *Saturday Review*, April 24, 1971, pp. 16–21.

23. *Reynolds v. United States*, 98 U.S. 145 (1878), sustaining the conviction of a Mormon for the crime of polygamy.

24. *Palo Alto Tenants Union v. Morgan*, 321 F. Supp. 908 (1970).

25. 381 U.S. 479 (1965).

26. *New York Times*, February 8, 1969, p. 29.

27. Simeon Booker, "The Couple That Rocked the Courts," *Ebony*, September, 1967, p. 78.

Suggestions for Further Reading

There are many interesting books for readers who wish to study the psychology and politics of race relations in more detail. Few of them are devoted to racial intermarriage alone—a recent exception is Joseph R. Washington, Jr., *Marriage in Black and White* (Boston: Beacon Press, 1970), a thoughtful analysis of arguments for and against by a clergyman who concludes that "the case for black-white unions is fundamentally the case for America." Most are general works dealing informatively with intermarriage in the context of intergroup relations or the rights of minorities. The following are some of the better examples.

On the subject of racial prejudice one might choose among Gordon W. Allport, *The Nature of Prejudice* (Cambridge, Mass.: Addison-Wesley, 1954), Bruno Bettelheim and Morris Janowitz, *The Dynamics of Prejudice* (New York: Harper, 1950), T. W. Adorno et al., *The Authoritarian Personality* (New York: Harper, 1950), and Joel Kovel, *White Racism: A Psychohistory* (New York: Pantheon, 1970), or read them all profitably. Milton Rokeach, *The Open and Closed Mind* (New York: Basic Books, 1960), relates racial attitudes to other kinds of prejudice in the course of reformulating the concept of authoritarianism.

Patterns of racial discrimination in the United States, including the intermarriage taboo, are described at length in Gunnar Myrdal, *An American Dilemma* (New York: Harper,

1944), still the definitive work. More recent insights are to be found in Thomas F. Pettigrew, *A Profile of the American Negro* (Princeton: Van Nostrand, 1964), with predictions of the long-run effects of miscegenation in the United States. For a more analytical treatment, see Hubert M. Blalock, Jr., *Toward a Theory of Minority Group Relations* (New York: John Wiley, 1967).

Any one of three recent volumes allows comparison of constraints on intermarriage, and other forms of racial discrimination, in the United States and other countries of the world: Pierre L. van den Berghe, *Race and Racism: A Comparative Prospect* (New York: John Wiley, 1967), John Hope Franklin, ed., *Color and Race* (Boston: Beacon Press, 1969), and Melvin Tumin, ed., *Comparative Perspectives on Race Relations* (Boston: Little, Brown, 1969).

On the legal and political side there are a number of interesting before and after studies of civil rights decisions of the Supreme Court. Clement E. Vose, *Caucasians Only: The Supreme Court, the NAACP, and the Restrictive Covenant Cases* (Berkeley: University of California Press, 1959), describes the successful efforts of civil rights lawyers to prepare a test case for consideration by the Court. Robert L. Crain, *The Politics of School Desegregation* (Chicago: Aldine, 1960), is a systematic study of the implementation of the public school desegregation decision, *Brown* v. *Board of Education.* Stephen L. Wasby, *The Impact of the United States Supreme Court* (Homewood, Ill.: Dorsey Press, 1970), provides a general analysis of the consequences of Supreme Court decisions.

For background information about the Supreme Court, see Archibald Cox, *The Warren Court* (Cambridge, Mass.: Harvard University Press, 1969), a brief, closely reasoned introduction to the thinking of the men who decided *Loving* v. *Virginia*—although it does not take up the *Loving* decision itself. Then, to explore the logical, prudential, and ideological underpinnings of the rulings of the Court, one may read Edward H. Levi, *An Introduction to Legal Reasoning* (Chicago: University of Chicago Press, 1948), Walter F. Murphy, *Elements of Judicial Strategy* (Chicago: University of Chicago Press, 1964), and Judith N. Shklar, *Legalism* (Cambridge, Mass.: Harvard University Press, 1964).

Finally, to keep abreast of developments in the law and practice of racial intermarriage, one may consult the federal and state court decisions cited in the latest volumes of the *General Digest* (St. Paul, Minn.: West), under "Marriage," sec. 4: "Persons who may marry," in a law library, and the tabulations of black-white marriages appearing two or three years after each decennial census in *United States Census*, Vol. PC(2)-4E: *Marital Status*, or its successors.

Index

Student Non-Violent Coordinating
    Committee, 131
Supreme Court of Appeals of Vir-
    ginia, 79, 81, 103-4
Supreme Court of the United States:
    strategy of, 7-9, 31, 88, 100

Taney, Roger B., 46, 92-93
Thurmond, Strom, 5
Truman, Harry S, 32

Uggams, Leslie, 124

UNESCO, 119
United Presbyterian Church, 61-62

Walker v. *Birmingham,* 5-6
Warren, Earl, 1, 6, 98, 102, 104,
    106-7
White, Walter S., 124
Wilkins, Roy, 87-88
Williams, Garth, 150
Wirth, Louis, 128
Wollenberg, Albert, 148-50
Wright, Richard, 124
Wulf, Melvin, 83